ON FIRE

ON FIRE

THE DRAMATIC RISE
OF THE CALGARY FLAMES

Eric Duhatschek & Steve Simmons

POLESTAR PRESS LTD.

ON FIRE

Published by

Polestar Press Ltd., R.R. 1, Winlaw, B.C., V0G 2J0 604-226-7670

Acknowledgements

The authors would like to thank the *Calgary Herald* for permission to use some previously published material. They would also like to acknowledge the assistance of senior assistant managing editor Gillian Steward; chief librarian Karen Liddiard and her staff; Molson's Alberta Breweries; the Calgary Flames' organization; Doug Smith of CFCN Television; reporter John Herbert of the *London Free Press*; and David, Daphne, and Matthew Taras.

Front-cover photo by Tom Walker.

Photo section and back-cover photo by Pat Price.

On Fire was produced by Polestar Press in Winlaw, B.C. and printed by Hignell Printers in Winnipeg in October, 1986.

Canadian Cataloguing in Publication Data

    Duhatschek, Eric, 1955 -
      On fire

    ISBN 0-919591-15-9

    1. Calgary Flames (Hockey team).
    I. Simmons, Steve, 1957 - II. Title.

GV848.C34D84 1986   796.96'26   C86-091546-8

This book is dedicated to Andreas and Katherina, to Jerry and Shirley, and to Mary and Sheila, who learned that hockey really is a twelve-month sport.

Contents

1
The Uncivil War

"There isn't a day that goes by that we don't think about the Calgary goal that beat us." WAYNE GRETZKY

On the day Steve Smith turned 23, the Edmonton Oilers' rookie defenceman gave the city of Calgary a long-awaited, much-anticipated birthday present. Unintentional. Unrehearsed. Unforgivable. In the seventh game of the Smythe Division final, at the Northlands Coliseum in Edmonton, with the score tied 2-2, Smith picked up the puck behind his own goal, took one step forward and banked a clearing pass off the back of goaltender Grant Fuhr's leg into his own net. "I got good wood on it," said Smith, smiling weakly. As it happened, Smith's goal — officially credited to Perry Berezan, the last Calgary player to handle the puck — turned out to be the Flames' margin of victory in what had become known as the Uncivil War, a fratricidal conflict between two cities and two teams that transcended a single game of ice hockey.

Even before there were Oilers and Flames, Calgary and Edmonton competed for the bragging rights to everything: football, baseball, rodeo, concert halls. You name it and people from Calgary and Edmonton fought over it. Moreover, in the

Smythe Division, the Oilers had been setting the standard for the last four years. For the Flames to get anywhere — today, tomorrow, 1999 — they needed to come up with a way of defeating Edmonton.

So it wasn't surprising that when the Flames scored the upset of the year in the year of the upset, the people in Edmonton found a convenient scapegoat in Smith. The dynasty died on the back of an untried rookie, they said. Since that fateful night, Smith's miscue has become a part of professional sports' rich history of blunders, but on the last day of April, 1986, no one in Calgary gave a damn about that. They had won. That's all that mattered.

All of the close calls, all of the what ifs, all the years of saying wait until next year dissolved in the afterglow of the victory. The Flames had received a present from heaven and took it with no questions asked. The deciding battle in an extraordinary war had ended on a quirky note, but that did nothing to temper the celebration 180 miles away down Highway 1.

The Flames took a charter flight to Calgary immediately after the game and were barely able to get home once they arrived. Their past playoff successes had fostered a tradition of airport greetings, but nothing compared to the crowd that met them following the series' win. Two games earlier, following the Flames' win in the fifth game, 3,000 fans packed themselves into an area designed to hold 500 people. So much damage was done that on the night the Flames won it all, their flight was diverted to the old airport terminal building. In a city of roughly half a million, 20,000 made their way to the airport, jamming every parking spot, pressing themselves up against the chain link fence, trying to catch a glimpse of the players as they descended from the aircraft.

The city partied all night. By dawn, seasons-ticket holders

were lined up to pay for their next batch of tickets. By 7 a.m., the box office opened to accommodate them. No one had seen anything like it before and no one expected to see anything like it again — even if the Flames went on to win the Stanley Cup. In the minds of many people, this *was* the Stanley Cup. Defeating the Oilers. In Edmonton. In the seventh game of a series. It had the flavour of Hollywood about it, such a clear measure of improbability that it took a few days for the achievement to sink in. And it didn't disappear until the season was long over. Indeed, the win — especially the remarkable way in which it had been won — marked the Flames as destiny's children. They were the highest-placed team remaining in the chase for the Stanley Cup. No reason on earth why they couldn't win it all now.

To understand the euphoria brought on by the Flames' dramatic win, it is necessary to go into the history of the rivalry between the two teams and the two cities. In Calgary, for the past three years, it seemed the only sure things in life were death, taxes, and the smirking, Cheshire grin on coach Glen Sather's face following another Oilers' win over the Flames. In that time, the Flames won two, lost nineteen and tied three in twenty-four regular-season games against the Oilers. Except for the 1984 playoff series, when the Flames pushed the Oilers to the edge, only to lose in the seventh game, this had become the most one-sided rivalry in hockey.

Understandably, the Oilers were having some trouble taking the Flames seriously. When the matter of the Flames-Oilers' rivalry came up for the umpteenth time during mid-season, the ever-cautious Wayne Gretzky politely suggested Calgary's main rivals had become the Winnipeg Jets because the Jets had eliminated them in the playoffs the year before and the Flames would be looking for a measure of revenge. Oilers-Flames? Hah. Gretzky, a discreet if timid interviewee, wouldn't be drawn into it. When the Flames did, as expected, brush the Jets aside in three games, the Oilers spent the better part of a week playing down the significance of the next series. They were, after all, the two-time defending Stanley Cup champions. They were, after all, the regular-season champions. They were, after all, thirty points better than the Flames.

They could, after all, afford to be confident. The recent history of games between the two teams showed the Oilers almost never had an off night against the Flames. Their heroes may have varied — Craig MacTavish stopped the Flames one night, Marty McSorley did them in in another — but the result was almost always the same. In six of eight regular-season games last year, the Flames found themselves behind 1-0 within six-and-a-half minutes. Twice they were down 1-0 within thirty seconds. For whatever reason — the Oilers' size, their confidence, their physical players — the Flames let themselves be intimidated by Edmonton's presence. They would alter their approach just enough to be uncomfortable for the start of every game. They would tighten up. They would freeze. They stopped thinking. In short, they played right into Edmonton's hands. Playing one way against the rest of the NHL and another way against the Oilers resulted in a frustrating series of losses. Some games were close. Some weren't. The only certainty was that when it was all over, the Oilers would emerge on top and the Flames would spend another night trying to explain what had happened.

Then there were the incidents. Over the years, almost every other game between the teams had turned into a free-for-all of some description. In the 1983-84 playoffs, the Oilers asked the NHL to investigate an incident in which Flames' centre Doug Risebrough clipped Oilers' right winger Glenn Anderson in the face with a high stick. Risebrough received a six-game suspension for his actions. The next season, the

Flames turned the tables on the Oilers, twice demanding that the league investigate Edmonton players for their attacks on Calgary players. The first time, Dave Semenko received a small fine for kneeing Steve Konroyd in the face during an altercation. The second time, Mark Messier received a ten-game suspension for a sneaky sucker-punch that knocked Flames' defenceman Jamie Macoun unconscious.

The most curious incident in the past season occurred during another routine, fight-filled Oilers' win in early January in Calgary. In the aftermath of a second-period brawl that saw five players ejected and 100 minutes in penalties assessed, Risebrough wound up in the penalty box with a sweater belonging to Oilers left winger Marty McSorley. Risebrough proceeded to shred the sweater into ribbons with his skate blades and then tossed it back onto the ice. When the game ended, Oilers' coach Glen Sather hung the sweater from the ceiling in the visitor's dressing room, called Risebrough's actions ''childish'' and told reporters he would bill the Flames for the damage.

The players were building up a real dislike for each other and so were the organizations. Flames' coach Bob Johnson and his Oilers' counterpart, Glen Sather, come from exactly opposite backgrounds. Sather came up the traditional way. A fringe player, he spent nine seasons with six different teams before joining the Oilers, then a member of the World Hockey Association, as a coach in 1977. He became the club's general manager and president following the 1980 season, Edmonton's first in the NHL. Johnson took a longer, more circuitous route to the NHL. His playing experience was limited to a couple of minor-league baseball teams. When his career stalled in 1956 with the Duluth Superiors of the Northern Baseball League, a Class C farm team of the Chicage White Sox, Johnson returned to the University of Minnesota to complete his physical education degree. He started coaching hockey by spending seven seasons in the Warroad, Minnesota high school system. In 1963, he moved up to the college ranks, joining Colorado College. Then he moved on to the University of Wisconsin, where he spent fifteen years. In that time, he won three national championships, finished second once and third twice.

Johnson came to the NHL as an anachronism, an American coaching in a game that Canadians had invented and sometimes thought they patented. Moreover, he was the first and only American coaching a Canadian-based team. He brought to the Flames a wealth of college and international experience, a hands-on approach to coaching that was supplemented by a good deal of outside study, but little that prepared him for the grind of an NHL season. In short, he was all the things that the average NHL coach wasn't.

The only area in which Sather and Johnson had anything in common was in their attitudes to motivation. But even there, their methods differed. Johnson's coaching philosophy didn't really change when he came to the NHL. As he saw it, there were two ways to coach — instilling fear in a player or instilling pride. Some coaches used fear to keep players in line. Johnson used pride.

"I maintain that to be a coach, you have to be a great teacher," Johnson once said. "You look at Don Shula, the great football coach or John Wooden (former basketball coach) at UCLA. They were all high-school teachers. Some people don't buy it. They think you have to be a former old pro to coach. Well, not when you're getting kids eighteen and nineteen that are still in the development stages and you've got to work with them on the fundamentals. You never have enough time to work with them, but you certainly do have some time. I believe in the value of practice. Some coaches don't. Some say you don't have to practice. That's the easy way out."

Sather's role differed. His owner, Peter Pocklington, secured him the most talented player in the game, Wayne Gretzky. His scouts loaded him down with five of the finest, purest talents in the league after Gretzky: Paul Coffey, Jari Kurri, Glenn Anderson, Mark Messier and Grant Fuhr. All along, his job differed from Johnson's — or from anyone else's for that matter. He needed to act as a broker for this collection of talent, keeping it in line, keeping the egos under control but not so far under wraps that they couldn't blossom on the ice. Of all the things said and written about Sather over the years, almost everybody misses his real strength as a coach. He is a master of manipulation. Sather could be George Orwell's model citizen in *1984*. He practically invented newspeak. In Sather's world, black is white, up is down, out is in and wrong is right. Sather is the only coach in history who could fortify his team with players like Marty McSorley, Jeff Brubaker, Dave Semenko, Dave Lumley and Don Jackson, then accuse other teams of employing goon tactics. He is the only coach in history who could unleash a vitriolic, personal attack on Johnson — calling into question his tactics, his nationality, his intelligence and his ring size — then turn around two days later and say he really liked the man.

As the teams prepared for their epic struggle, no one did more than Sather to exacerbate the conflict. Johnson, a slave to coaching gimmicks, was using one in the days preceeding the first game. Johnson dressed his two practice goaltenders, Jamie Bowman of Calgary Canucks and Al Hryniuk of the University of Calgary, in Oilers' sweaters. Johnson, in explaining his move, said he wanted his players to get used to the idea of shooting at Oilers' goalies.

Sather flipped. Insisting he didn't want to get drawn into a war of words with the Flames, he proceeded to stir the pot anyway. ''Johnson putting two goalies out there in practice wearing Oilers' uniforms,'' said Sather, warming up to the subject, ''if you honestly think that's going to have any effect on their players or on our players, you totally underestimate the intelligence of the modern player. We're not talking about a bunch of kids who come out of back streets. These are intelligent people, well-paid, well-trained, well-conditioned people. A lot of them are very well educated. I've never seen this tactic before. It's strange. It must be something you learn in college in the U.S. Of course, he is American. I guess he thinks differently than I do. Me, I'm Canadian-born, in Alberta, High River as a matter of fact; not far from Calgary. I probably think more logically than he does. If you think it'll have an effect on how McDonald shoots because he sees somebody in an Oiler sweater in practice, forget it. That's just hype.''

Just how Sather thought Calgary would react to his speech — it sounded as if he was claiming some kinship with the city that Johnson would never have — wasn't clear. Johnson, given the chance to respond, wouldn't. Of all the brushfires that were blazing by then, the one he least wanted to get drawn into was a war of words with his opposite number.

Apart from cracking that he could ''just see Sather wrapping himself up in the (Canadian) flag,'' Johnson begged off the conflict. He called the war of words ''a one-way street,'' but he couldn't resist the odd, subtle dig.

''What have we ever said about them?'' asked Johnson. ''Seriously? I've never said a thing about them. I don't think in my whole coaching career I've ever said anything about the other coach. You don't serve anything by that. Glen Sather wants the edge. He's no different than other coaches. He has been very successful because he has had the edge up to now and he doesn't want to give it up. He has a great edge in Gretzky. What kind of a coach would he be with another team? Have you ever thought of that? So I know what he's trying to do. He has done a good job with the chemistry of their club, but he has always tried to stay ahead of everybody else. So far, he has.''

Others were less cautious than Johnson. Dave Lumley, a part-time Oiler, couldn't understand the ''complex'' that the city of Calgary had developed about Edmonton: ''All we've got is the Oilers, the Eskimos and West Edmonton Mall. But I guess all they've got is a nickname — and you can have Cowtown.'' Marty McSorley, a member of the Oilers' protection racket, said: ''Calgary has big strong guys who present problems. The potential for war is there. But the big guys aren't going to decide this series. And we don't pay any attention to all the stories. Personally, I'm going to be very aware of not going out and taking a bad penalty or making a bad giveaway. We know that if we play at the top of our game, we'll win, that's all.''

Somehow, the word ''war'' kept coming up. Risebrough said the Flames knew they had a ''war'' on their hands, that they were ready and anxious to do battle. Then he explained that by war, he meant the possibility of seven back-to-back games that would lead to a series that was extremely hard-fought. On the ice.

From a Flames' perspective, defenceman Paul Reinhart explained the rivalry better than anyone. Said Reinhart: ''The games against Edmonton are important because everything we do from September to April will always be compared to and plotted against how Edmonton did. They're the ones we have to catch. If you win seventy-two games in a year and lose eight to them and then lose again in the playoffs, then where are you? Nowhere. We could fool ourselves and say we're trying to catch the Washington Capitals, but that's not what we're trying to do. We're trying to catch Edmonton. They're the mark we compare ourselves to. When all is said and done,

17

that's what it comes down to; all the trades, all the talk, everything we do.''

So when Berezan's unassisted goal 5:14 into the third period gave the Flames the deciding battle in the Uncivil War, it proved to be almost too much for the players to put into words.

The play began innocently enough, with Berezan dumping the puck into the Oilers' zone, then heading to the bench for a line change. As he reached the bench, the Northlands Coliseum became suddenly quiet. ''I turned and I saw Lanny with his hands in the air,'' said Berezan. ''I had to ask him what happened.'' McDonald told him. ''Sometimes,'' said McDonald, ''the good Lord smiles on you.''

Until the winning goal, the seventh game had followed a familiar playoff pattern. The Flames took the lead. The Oilers tied it. In the third period, the game was up for grabs. Berezan's goal swung the momentum from the Oilers to the Flames, proving once again that in an all-or-nothing showdown, anything can happen... and usually does.

The Flames almost allowed the Oilers to get back into it as time ran out. The first time, defenceman Neil Sheehy nearly duplicated Smith's feat, almost putting a pass behind goaltender Mike Vernon. The second time, the Flames were caught with too many men on the ice in the last minute, giving the Oilers — who pulled goaltender Grant Fuhr — a six-on-four advantage in skaters. This time, however, luck smiled on the Flames. When Sheehy and Vernon played Keystone Cops in the crease, Vernon had the presence of mind to cover the puck. When Jari Kurri passed instead of shooting on the Oilers only legitimate scoring chance, the Flames were able to ice the puck without stopping play.

Later, in the dressing room bedlam, Vernon said: ''I've waited all year for this and now it's happened. You know my story. Everybody knows my story by now. It's a great feeling. I'm glad to be part of beating Edmonton. I'm a Calgarian. There's nothing that I wanted more than to beat Edmonton, except to win the Stanley Cup.''

''This isn't just for Calgary,'' said Lanny McDonald. ''This is for everybody. This is for the oilmen. This is for the oldtimers. This is for the wives and children. To know you've knocked off the Stanley Cup champions. Yeaaaaaah. It's fabulous. I don't even think it's hit us yet. It'll hit us tomorrow.''

For the Flames, the turning point in the season ultimately came in the last two regular-season meetings with the Oilers, a 4-4 tie and a 9-3 win. The Oilers brushed them off as a pair of nothing games. Perhaps that was a lesson: when you're the champions, there is no such thing as a nothing game. In retrospect, they may have been the Oilers' two most important regular-season games — though they had no way of knowing it at the time.

Not only did the Flames shed a Kong-sized monkey from their backs, they began to believe, really believe, that the Oilers were vulnerable. Ever since Johnson's arrival in Calgary, he compared the struggle to catch Edmonton to climbing a mountain. In the fourth year of his stewardship, the Flames finally completed the conquest of Mount Oiler.

Only one development dampened the celebration that night. In the first period, defenceman Gary Suter took a hit from Oilers' centre Mark Messier and twisted his knee. Suter sat on the bench for the second period and didn't play a shift. In the third, he took a shower. Messier's hit severed the ligaments in his left knee. The run to the Stanley Cup was just beginning, but Suter's season was over.

It would prove to be a costly loss.

ON FIRE

2
The Battle of Alberta

"We didn't expect to beat them four straight."

JOEY MULLEN

Cliff Fletcher paced anxiously, speaking just loudly enough so everyone could hear. ''He was skewered,'' said Fletcher. Then he repeated himself, in case members of the media hadn't heard him the first time. ''I tell you, he was skewered,'' he said, the morning after the Flames had dropped game six to the Oilers. ''If you want to see the films, I'll show you.'' Fletcher moved like a nervous cat, darting up and down the corridor behind the Flames bench at the Olympic Saddledome. He was angry, upset, uptight, confused, but mostly nervous. The Flames should have beaten the Oilers by now. The seven game series should have been over in six. But it wasn't. So there was the Flames' president and general manager, trying to create an issue, trying to divert attention, trying to take the pressure off a hockey club under pressure. He found his *cause celebre* in centre Carey Wilson, who earlier that morning had lost his spleen on an operating table, the result of a hit the night before. Wilson was finished for the playoffs.

Fletcher pointed his finger at Oilers' defenceman Steve

20

Smith, whom he accused of spearing Wilson. By this time, reporters were beginning to congregate around Fletcher, sensing a new chapter in the ''war of words'' story. Fletcher's complaining sounded interesting, especially considering the wall of secrecy the Flames had constructed around the press corps throughout the playoffs. When a group of reporters finally gathered in Bob Johnson's office following practice, they asked to see the ''skewer'' on videotape. Assistant coach Pierre Page obliged. Winding and rewinding the tape with his remote control, Page found the ''incident.'' Slowly he backed the tape up. ''Here it is,'' he said. Then he showed the play which involved Wilson and Smith. It didn't look violent. It didn't look deliberate. It didn't look like much. It certainly didn't look like the aforementioned skewer, described only a few minutes ago in such aggressive tones.

The war of words ended on that note. Only one game remained. Centre Carey Wilson was out. Smith, who later became the goat of Game 7, was branded as the goon of Game 6 — even though his collision with Wilson appeared harmless on tape. But it was only after Wilson returned from hospital weeks later that the truth came out. Curious about what had happened to himself, Wilson took to the back of the Flames' dressing room to check out the game films on his own. After several minutes of watching tape, he emerged with a smile. ''I found it,'' he said. It wasn't Smith at all. It turned out Wilson had been injured by a Charlie Huddy cross-check, a move that didn't even warrant a penalty. So much for the skewering incident. So much for the verbal war which both infected and promoted the series before and after each clash. But when the games began, the words became secondary.

It didn't take long for people to realize what was happening. The series unfolded as a drama on skates: emotion, excitement, passion, intensity, action. Every game seemed better than the last one. No one wanted it to end. You couldn't ask for more and the players couldn't give any more. Sometimes, you had to blink to make sure it was all real. The balletic ability of Grant Fuhr. The dexterity of Gretzky. The true grit of Doug Risebrough. Sometimes you had to stop, to make sure your emotions hadn't carried you away. It took just a few series' games for the comparisons to begin. Which series was greater? The battle of Alberta or the battle of New York? Where did this series place historically? Alberta had its own provincial version of the Canada-Soviet Summit Series of 1972, but the battles were not ideological.

The Oilers were Goliath and the Flames David. The Oilers had Gretzky, the Flames didn't. The experts assumed the Smythe Division final would be an interesting series, not a long one. There were simply too many obstacles to be overcome. Too many matchups which didn't match. Too many variables which favoured Edmonton. But then the puck was dropped, and the words and stories froze in time. This could have been a novel written by Ludlum, unpredictable in its beginning, middle and end. This could have been an action film, which never slowed in pace or plot.

When the first game began, it didn't take long for one point to become apparent: plain and simple, Edmonton would have to beat the Flames to win the series. The Flames were not about to beat themselves. That was proven in Game 1. It took Lanny McDonald just eighty-seven seconds into the series to give the Flames their first lead. After Gary Suter made it 2-0 some six minutes later, the Oilers looked confused by the Flames: by the standup goaltending of Mike Vernon, by the third man back on defence, by the line matchups. Joey Mullen and Hakan Loob scored Calgary's other goals in a 4-1 win. Glenn Anderson scored for Edmonton.

"One win doesn't prove anything," said Suter, a first-game star. ''We've got three more to go.''

Overlooked in the excitement of Game 1 was a brilliant save by Vernon that would cause him problems after the game. The Oilers' star defenceman Paul Coffey had skated in on a breakaway, made one move, then another, and appeared to have the young goaltender deked, when all of a sudden Vernon moved to his right and made Coffey miss. Vernon continued. It wasn't until the next day he learned how badly his knee had been injured. The Flames didn't practise with Vernon on the day between games, and the young goaltender spent most of his time in the jacuzzi and taking treatment. When he walked, he tried to hide the limp, and when asked how he was, he hid the truth as well. While the Flames were obviously going to make one lineup change with Vernon out, the Oilers were preparing for some surprises of their own. If the Flames had managed anything other than a victory in the first game, it was the fact they wiped the smile off Sather's face. Sather looked all business as he ran the Oilers' workout the next day and that sent a message to his players. In the past, when things went well with the Oilers, Sather left the practice sessions to co-coach John Muckler. When times were troubled, Slats would come to the rescue.

Thinking the Oilers were pushed around too much in Game 1, Sather devised a plan for Game 2. Push back. He inserted Dave Lumley, who had only played once in the past six weeks, in place of winger Marty McSorley. Raimo Summanen went in for another Finnish winger Esa Tikkanen. And Don Jackson took Steve Smith's place on the Oilers defence. But that wasn't all. Feeling that Gretzky was ineffective in the opener, Sather planned to find more room for him. His method: move lumbering Dave Semenko to the line that also included Jari Kurri. Lumley, who plays from the heart and with the stick, was to join Anderson and Mark Messier. And Sather put together a line based on size, using Mike Krushelnyski with Kevin McClelland.

"We're not planning any line changes," coach Muckler said between games. "We do this all the time." Muckler's words proved one thing. Co-coaches can be as deceptive as head coaches. The next night, the Oilers lined up with all the changes they had used in Saturday's workout. Who said honesty is the best policy?

On Sunday morning, the day of Game 2, Mike Vernon limped through the lobby of the Four Seasons Hotel in Edmonton. "How do you feel?" he was asked. "No problem," he said, unconvincingly. But Reggie Lemelin, the forgotten man, would start in goal. Vernon had played against Edmonton three times that season, beating them twice, tying them once. For all the great goal Lemelin had played as a Flame, little of it came against the Oilers. It was never clear whether he psyched himself out against the Oilers, but one thing was painfully clear: it wasn't one of the teams he controlled.

Again, as was to be their custom in the playoffs, the Flames scored first. If more interesting games than this one had been played before, few had ever witnessed them. This was a classic. It featured a large lead, a comeback, an overtime goal, a fluky goal and a fight in the stands. All of which was tightly packaged into sixty-one minutes and four seconds of hockey.

Flames' assistant trainer Al Murray was standing behind the bench in his usual position when defenceman Gary Suter was checked into the boards. Suter escaped, but his stick did not. The aluminum stick wound up in the fourth row of seats at the Northlands Coliseum. Murray, not thinking of the Calgary-Edmonton rivalry, leapt from the bench into the stands to retrieve Suter's stick. Murray grabbed it, but the fan holding it wouldn't let go. A fight broke out, not on the ice, but between fan and assistant trainer. Seeing that his son appeared to have his hands full, Flames' trainer Bearcat Murray attempted to jump over the glass to come to his boy's rescue. Bearcat didn't return healthy. Landing on the glass with his right foot, Murray injured his ankle. It turned out to be Game 2's most serious injury. The next day he was on crutches, nursing torn ligaments.

On the ice, Grant Fuhr had made one of his few mistakes of the series to give the Flames the lead. With the game tied in the second period, Calgary's Dan Quinn redirected a shot from outside the Oilers' blueline in Fuhr's direction. Fuhr was playing Michael Jackson, wearing a glove for no apparent reason. He allowed the puck to slide under his mitt and into the net and the Flames led 3-2. The goal may have foreshadowed what was to come in the series. No matter what the Flames did, they seemed destined to win. Fuhr looked at his glove, as if it had let him down, then turned around, pounded on the net, and went on with the game.

The dribbler which beat Fuhr gave the Flames a lift. Mullen quickly followed Quinn's goal with one of his own, and Calgary led 4-2 with one period to play. Even Lemelin, with so much past difficulty against the Oilers, was holding up his end of the bargain. It looked as though Calgary was going to accomplish the impossible: sweep the first two games of the series in Edmonton. But when the third period began, Sather decided not to start the Gretzky line or the Messier line. Countering Sather's moves, Johnson matched his defence pairs against the Oilers' lines, trying to get speed against speed, but it didn't work. When the Oilers began with centre Craig MacTavish's line, the Flames used Neil Sheehy and Terry Johnson on defence. With Al MacInnis absent because of a bruised foot that occurred in Game 1, the Flames were playing without their top defencemen. Paul Reinhart, Jamie Macoun and Gary Suter gave them three high-quality NHL defencemen. MacInnis was to be the fourth. Now he was out. The Flames would have to live and die with Sheehy, Johnson, and Paul Baxter.

As it turned out, they did a little of both. When the period began, MacTavish had the puck within seconds. He raced past one Flame, and walked around the plodding Johnson, then Lemelin, to put the puck in the net. From there on, it was almost all Oilers. The 4-2 lead dissipated. Quickly the Oilers had gone ahead 5-4. The series was about to be tied. That is, until Mullen scored his second goal of the game, knocking a puck down with his glove beside the Oilers' goal, shooting it into the net in one quick motion to send the game into overtime. But overtime didn't last long. The Oilers just kept coming. Lumley, playing his first game in so long, made the key play on the winning goal by Anderson at 1:04 of overtime. The series was now tied. It was time to return to Calgary.

Said Mullen after the disillusioning loss: "We didn't expect to beat them four straight."

With the series tied 1-1, Wayne Gretzky looked in the mirror and didn't like what he saw. He saw himself two games into the Smythe Division final without so much as a goal. What worried Gretzky was his lack of production. What worried the Flames was Gretzky's dormancy. How long would it be before he would explode? Gretzky, always his harshest critic, put added pressure upon himself when he wasn't producing. Already he had heard the rumors and the questions. Was he injured? Was something wrong? Linemate Kurri attempted to take the pressure off The Great One. Kurri himself took the blame for the lack of productivity on hockey's highest scoring line. "Wayne isn't getting any help from me," said Kurri. "I'm brutal. I keep finding myself in places where I can't even score. I just don't feel that good."

Back in the Flames' camp, Mike Vernon was starting to

feel just fine. Vernon returned to the goal on Tuesday night, in time to start Game 3. As well as he played that night, fans left the Saddledome talking about the goaltender at the other end, Fuhr. This was to be another proving night to the Flames, and they proved for the third straight time they could outplay the Oilers. They could not, however, solve the mystery of Fuhr. Just a few nights ago, Fuhr had let a dribbler by him, but there were no gifts this time. Fuhr somehow, marvellously, miraculously, got a glove or a pad in the way of so many shots which seemed able to score. It was Drydenesque goaltending. But it still wasn't enough to beat the Flames, who made one roster move of significance in the game. Coach Johnson shifted winger Jim Peplinski to centre, giving the Flames four centres of substantial size and strength to play against the Oilers. With Peplinski moving off his line, his old centreman Joel Otto combined with Mullen to score the winning goal in the Flames 3-2 victory. Game 3 was thought to be the pivotal game. The team that won that game would win the series, people thought. As it turned out, after each game was played, that held true. The team that won the next game would win the series. It carried right through, until there was just one game left to play.

The Flames appeared loose heading into Game 1, and then tight once they took the lead. That pattern continued throughout most of the series. They were fine when they had to win, not so fine when a win would put them comfortably ahead. They didn't get too high after a win or too low after a loss. There was no comfort zone in the series. Not as long as Fuhr continued to play the way he was playing. Not as long as Gretzky remained an Oiler. The questions of Gretzky's well-being continued. Rumors circulated that he had a fight with his girlfriend. Others thought he had a knee problem or a shoulder problem. Surely, something must have been wrong. Three games into the series he still hadn't scored, but it was only a matter of time.

The worst nightmares of the Flames were realized in Game 4. To chants of ''whiner, whiner'' Gretzky responded. He turned the red light on, quieting the Saddledome fans dressed in red. They couldn't stop Gretzky with a howitzer. The fans may have come dressed in red, but they left feeling blue. The Flames had found themselves in a shooting match with the Oiler pool sharks. And they lost everything that night, from the game to the fights. Gretzky set up the game's first goal and scored the second, his first of the series. He set up the Oilers third goal and scored their fifth. That was all the Oilers needed, really, in a 7-4 win. A win that turned ugly in the final period. The Flames' tough guy Tim Hunter fought Semenko and Tikkanen and Krushelnyski. Newcomer Nick Fotiu danced around a lot, wasted time, and fought no one. On that night he went from fan favourite to fan target. It seemed everyone fought anyone they could get their hands on, and all of it had nothing to do with the result which was rather one-sided. In all, referee Bob Myers called 196 minutes in penalties in a game he lost control of. The Flames were not only beaten, they were beaten up.

Lanny McDonald went to sleep disappointed and woke up angry. He was mad because the Oilers had taken back home ice advantage. He was mad because the Flames' power play hadn't cashed in the night before. ''We know damn well we had the chance to go ahead 3-1. It's not just disappointing to the fans, it's disappointing to us.''

McDonald wasn't the only one who felt that way. Vernon was angry too. Pulled after Gretzky's second goal the night before, he couldn't think of anything except coming back, beating the Oilers. The loss in Game 4 was his first in almost two NHL months. ''I have to bounce back,'' he said. ''John Vanbiesbrouck did it in the Rangers series. I can't let it get me down.''

The calls poured in to Don Hudson's CBC phone-in show on Friday afternoon. ''I want to know your predictions on the series,'' Hudson asked his listeners. And when the hour was up, the verdict was in. The Flames had given it their all, but the series was over. Edmonton would go home for Game 5, win, then win one of the final two games of the series. That's the way it would go, most callers thought. That seemed to be the conventional thinking, but if the Smythe Division final proved anything, it was that conventional thinking could be obsolete. Worried about Vernon's confidence, Fuhr's ability, Gretzky's momentum and the inevitable outbreak of Paul Coffey, the Flames travelled wearily back to Edmonton. For a brief while their fans may have lost faith. Somehow, the team did not.

Gretzky didn't skate out when his name was called as the game's third star. That had never happened before, but Gretzky and the Oilers hadn't been in this position before. In the final seconds of Game 5, a frustrated Gretzky tossed his stick along the ice knocking the puck into an empty net. The goal was awarded to Doug Risebrough. Afterwards, Gretzky was dressed and out of the Oiler dressing room much faster than usual. The unexpected had again happened. The Flames were again ahead. Down the hall at Northlands, the Flames dressing room was a mass of jubilation. ''I have nothing against the city of Edmonton,'' said Jim Peplinski. ''I just have no desire to come back here again.'' Neither did the rest of his teammates. The Flames were a victory away from beating the Stanley Cup champions. There was a cure for Edmonton's hat trick fever of winning three straight Cups. Take two aspirins and call the Flames in the morning.

Game 5, as much as any game, mirrored the series itself. It had novelistic twists and changing strategies and everything in the end seemed to work for the Flames. The game was a series of short storms: the Flames would take a lead, the Oilers would come back appearing to be stronger. Vernon again bounced back from an ordinary fourth game to a marvellous fifth. When he wasn't great, he was lucky and when he wasn't lucky he was damned good.

If the fans in Calgary had only slightly lost faith after Game 4, the players had not. Neither had the club's owners. Prior to the game Norm Green, one of the Flames' six owners, predicted his club would win. On his cab-ride to the Coliseum that night, the driver wanted to bet Green on the evening's outcome. Green wanted to bet $1. The taxi driver wanted to bet $100. "I don't want to take your money," said Green. "But I think the Flames will win, 5-4." They bet the $1 on the game. Green left his dollar and his business card with the cab driver, who was surprised to see he was one of the Flame owners. Green won his bet, but he never saw that dollar again.

The Oilers were again in an unfamiliar position — they were behind. And again, they promised to claw their way out. After the shocking loss of Game 5, Oiler players sat silently, wondering what had gone wrong. Kevin Lowe, the stay-at-home defenceman who doubles as chief Oiler spokesman in two languages, said that it was time for a refresher course in modern Oiler history. "Whenever we've needed to win a game in the last two years, we've won it. It happened in the regular season. When we said to ourselves, 'Fellas, we want to win this game,' we did." But it didn't seem to make sense. Why hadn't they done what was previously so easy for them? "There just wasn't the same feeling. We'll have that feeling for Game 6."

As flamboyant as Oilers' owner Peter Pocklington is, he has never been known as an interfering owner. Normally, he left the business of hockey to Sather and his staff. But once in a while, he flexed his chest, pulled out his best inspirational speech, and headed towards the dressing room. On the Oilers' first run to the Stanley Cup, Pocklington once showed up at practice. When asked why he was at practice, his answer was: "To make sure there are more practices." The Oilers won the next night, and never looked back. And now, trailing 3-2 in the series, it was time for Pocklington to make another appearance in the Oilers' dressing room. A loss would not only eliminate his club, but cost him into the millions of dollars in potential revenue. A loss wasn't something he wanted to afford and he stated so in no uncertain terms.

Pocklington wasn't alone in his pleas. Sather, too, had been frustrated by his team. He attempted to alter his game plan, but the players did not adapt accordingly. He wanted them to begin dumping the puck over the blue line and chasing it, playing mortal hockey, instead of their normally artistic game. He had allowed them to digress into a state of infallibility, and now, when he needed it most, there was nothing he could do. Sather had become his own worst enemy. No matter what he told his team, it didn't seem to sink in. The Oilers, who became champions playing one style, refused to adapt to another. It proved to be their ultimate downfall.

The champagne was on ice at the Saddledome on April 28, in anticipation of a Flames victory, but the bottles went unopened. The ice turned slowly to water. It was all there for the Flames' taking: the champagne, the celebration, the Smythe Division title. Five years of frustration were ready to come to an end. But instead, it continued. The Flames had appeared poised to end the Oilers' two-year domination. They had talked about breaking the barrier of Fuhr the magnificent, but again could not solve the mystery. The more pressure the Flames applied, the better Fuhr got. He wouldn't let the Oilers lose, not yet. Strangely, the Edmonton reaction following the

5-2 sixth game victory was one of relief. They had dodged another bullet and they knew it. The Flames, surprisingly, were not in the state of emotional flux that might have been expected.

In his office, Bob Johnson anxiously answered the post-game questions. Yes, he knew the Flames had chances to win the game and end the series. No, the series wasn't over. All along, through his speeches on mountain climbing, his golf analogies, his odd practice methods, and his general paranoia, Johnson had maintained one pose. He wanted to shorten the series to a best-of-one. "The shorter the series, the better chance we have," he'd say. Finally, Johnson had his wish. The Flames had lost Game 6. It was now a 60-minute series.

3
Lanny

"People keep talking about my age, but I feel good. I don't feel old." LANNY McDONALD

In his dream, the teen-age Lanny McDonald circles the ice, his blue-and-white uniform drenched with perspiration and champagne, the heel of his hand on the base of the Stanley Cup as the scrum of hockey players moves like a living thing around the ice at Maple Leaf Gardens. In his dream, McDonald is clean-shaven and in the uniform of the Toronto Maple Leafs. In 1973, no one could predict the world-famous moustache nor the fact that the Edmonton Oilers would supplant the Leafs as Canada's team. The Calgary Flames? They were eight years, four thousand miles and several near-bankruptcies away from existence.

Times changed. Years passed. By the time the 1985-86 season began, McDonald was starting his fourth year with his third NHL team, wondering if the dream, even a modified version, would ever come alive. McDonald spent all of the Flames' pre-season telling people he wasn't ready for the scrap heap, trying to show there was enough life left in his thirty-two-year-old legs to produce another effective season.

He made some extraordinary forecasts in September: that he could play every day; that he could survive a season injury-free; that he could score fifty goals; that he and his teammates could maybe, just maybe, give the Edmonton Oilers a run for their money in the playoffs. Much of it sounded improbable. Some of it sounded impossible.

Under close scrutiny, the greying of Lanny McDonald had become apparent. It was evident on the sides and in the back and even if the perpetually tousled red hair hid the fine white lines from longer range, McDonald was clearly getting on in years. Then came the more tangible proof. Darryl Sittler was gone and Tiger Williams was going and because, for better or worse, the trio will always be linked in people's minds as a result of their years with the Leafs, it was logical to think McDonald would be next.

Injuries limited him to forty-three frustrating games and nineteen goals the year before, his lowest total since the 1974-75 season and the first time he failed to score thirty goals in ten years. He needed to put behind him a knee operation that followed a lengthy convalescence from pulled stomach muscles that followed a broken foot. He needed to stay healthy and he needed to stop the slide in his goalscoring from sixty-six to thirty-three to nineteen that occurred in a span of twenty-four months. His enthusiasm was admirable and it was catching. If only the legs could keep up.

Perhaps the quality that set McDonald apart from others with similar pipedreams was that he never lost his child-like love for the game. Unlike many players, McDonald's public face accurately mirrored his private self. There really wasn't anything he would rather do than come to the arena and play the game. They used to talk about players who would play for free if the professional leagues didn't exist. McDonald is one. His identity is tied so closely to ice hockey that it is difficult to foresee a day when he isn't coming back for one more season with the Flames.

By the start of the new season, even coach Bob Johnson had some misgivings. When he heard about McDonald's pre-season goals, Johnson praised him for his positive thinking, but made it clear he thought fifty goals would be unrealistic. The Flames had spent the previous summer combing the league for the player McDonald had been, the big scorer. When they failed to bring one in, McDonald took it upon himself to become that player again. Johnson thought it would be enough that McDonald played and contributed, on and off the ice.

"Age," said McDonald, "would not be an issue. You need a drive and desire to stay in the game at a competitive level. People keep talking about my age, but I feel good. I don't feel old. I feel young. Playing the game helps keep me young. I'm in better shape now than I was last year or the year before. I don't think that I'm a step behind or anything.

"What better way to show people how you feel than to go out and prove it to them eighty times a year and twenty more times in the playoffs. That's about what it takes to win the Stanley Cup, isn't it?"

Things couldn't have started worse for McDonald. Ten days into training camp, he dislocated the thumb on his right hand, the hand he uses to give his shot that extra snap. For the rest of the exhibition season and for the first month, McDonald couldn't shoot properly. The only positive development was that he stopped worrying about his other problems. McDonald worked on his conditioning and his skating and found his knee was more secure than he thought. For the season opener against the Winnipeg Jets, doctors put a cast on his thumb enabling McDonald to play.

The minor injuries continued. McDonald started the year by aggravating his knee. Next he injured his hip. Then he came down with a severe case of the flu. Then he stopped shots on both his ankles. No bones were broken, but he spent a couple of weeks hobbling up and down the right side of the ice. Through it all, McDonald didn't miss a game. Even he couldn't explain why, on a night when he had a 101 degree temperature, he played against the New York Islanders. Pride had something to do with it. Had it been the New Jersey Devils, maybe he'd have taken the night off, but McDonald wouldn't bail out of a game against the Islanders.

He wondered at the time if he'd "ever play healthy again" and he was discouraged enough to predict that probably he wouldn't. Even if it affected his day — and it did — he wouldn't divulge the seriousness of the injuries or their effect on his play. He said nothing, forcing people to draw their own conclusions. Some people, even in the upper echelons of the team's management, started wondering how much McDonald had left.

The story of Lanny McDonald's acquisition by the Flames began midway through the 1974-75 season when general manager Cliff Fletcher, then of the Atlanta Flames, almost pried him away from the Toronto Maple Leafs — for journeyman Curt Bennett. Fletcher's plan was to unite the struggling McDonald with centre Tom Lysiak, his junior linemate and the Flames' most accomplished player. McDonald, then in his third year with the Leafs, wasn't living up to expectations. He came to Toronto amid high hopes for a Maple Leafs' turnaround. The fourth player selected in the 1973 amateur draft, McDonald was young, strong, and could score goals. He looked like he had all the right stuff to play in the hockey capital of Canada. For the Leafs, choosing McDonald was supposed to be like buying stock in Xerox, a sure thing.

It didn't turn out that way. Not immediately. Two-and-a-half years into his pro career, McDonald was a gangly and confused player and the Leafs were losing patience. As Fletcher waited in the wings, trying to steal this blue-chip prospect away, things slowly started to come around for McDonald. Indeed, just as Fletcher and his Toronto counterpart Jim Gregory tentatively agreed the deal would go through, McDonald began to score. He scored two goals one night, one goal the next and the Leafs started having second thoughts. The decision to wait became one of their most astute non-moves ever.

As for Fletcher, he needed another seven years to complete the deal for McDonald. The trade finally happened on November 26, 1981 when the Flames gave up two of their most popular players, Don Lever and Bob MacMillan, to the Colorado Rockies to get McDonald.

Much had happened in the interim. McDonald had been traded to Colorado during the Christmas season of 1979 at the height of a player rebellion against Punch Imlach, the man who replaced Gregory as Toronto's general manager. Suddenly, the most interesting things about the Leafs weren't what they did on the ice, but what they did off the ice.

McDonald and Sittler had become two of the finest young players in the game by then. In 1976, Sittler, assisted by McDonald, scored the overtime goal that allowed Canada to defeat Czechoslovakia and win the inaugural Canada Cup. Two years later, the Leafs upset the Islanders in overtime in the seventh game of the Stanley Cup quarter-finals, with McDonald scoring the winner on Chico Resch. They were on their way to the top. Or so it appeared.

Less than two years later, the bottom had fallen out. Imlach didn't like Sittler but couldn't trade him. Gregory had given Sittler a no-trade contract and Sittler refused to go in the general housecleaning that Imlach had planned. So Imlach, trying to break up the team he inherited, traded McDonald instead. Some thought he moved McDonald to get back at Sittler. Even Sittler isn't sure to this day if that's what happened. The day after the trade, Sittler resigned as the Leafs' captain moments before a nationally televised game. The camera picked up the threads of the lettering on his sweater where he'd ripped off the C.

McDonald, meanwhile, was on his way to Colorado, leaving behind a pregnant wife, a brand new house, and a team that he thought was getting closer all the time to challenging for the Stanley Cup. Instead, he joined the Rockies, a dead-end collection of players who believed making the playoffs qualified as a major achievement. Stanley Cups were for the next century, the next incarnation of the franchise. So McDonald spent the next three years in Denver, learning to love the city and hate the losses that came night after disheartening night.

In Colorado, the Rockies were under pressure to make the playoffs in the weak Smythe Division in the 1981-82 season. They were playing poorly, but so were the Flames, the Los Angeles Kings, and the Vancouver Canucks. Nobody was out of it. Rockies' general manager Bill MacMillan thought two quality NHLers such as Lever and Bobby MacMillan, his younger brother, would do more for the team than one McDonald could. So on the November night that they lost a game to the Flames in Calgary, MacMillan dropped McDonald into Fletcher's lap. The move caught McDonald completely off guard. Just days before, MacMillan had said McDonald wasn't available, that a team — no matter how badly off it was — needed cornerstones. His words proved prophetic. McDonald became a cornerstone — in Calgary. Two years later, the Rockies were in New Jersey and Billy MacMillan was looking for work.

To understand McDonald's state of mind approaching the

1986 playoffs, one needed to look no further than the men sitting beside him on the players' bench. One was his centre, Doug Risebrough, a winner of four Stanley Cup championships with the Montreal Canadiens, the embodiment of what it takes to be a winner. The other was left winger John Tonelli, a member of four Stanley Cup championship teams with the New York Islanders and a player with the same characteristics as Risebrough. Among his other contributions, Tonelli was the team's playoff MVT — most valuable talker. From the day he arrived, he started talking up the Stanley Cup: how to win it and what it felt like to win it. Much of it was done for the benefit of the team's younger players, but the speech had its effect on McDonald as well. He knew that time was running out on his career. He knew the team was gradually picking itself up after its eleven consecutive losses. He saw the changes made by Fletcher starting to take effect. When the playoffs began, the Flames' players had talked themselves into believing that this could be their year.

When McDonald originally joined the Flames in 1981, the team was in disarray. General manager Cliff Fletcher was in the midst of dissecting a team that had gone to the Stanley Cup semifinals the year before. By the time McDonald had arrived, the Flames were in the bottom third of the league and trying desperately to replace a cast of players that wanted no part of Calgary.

Moreover, the beginnings of a shift in the league's power base had started, one that would have significant repercussions in Calgary. The Edmonton Oilers, one of the youngest teams in the league and a refugee from the defunct World Hockey Association, were showcasing the NHL's finest young player, Wayne Gretzky. Slowly, the Oilers were building a team out of the scraps they were left with when they joined the NHL.

In McDonald's first year in Calgary, the Oilers won the

Smythe Division crown going away, but lost to Los Angeles in the playoffs. In McDonald's second year, the Oilers made the finals. In McDonald's third year, they won the Cup. In his fourth year, they won it again.

The Oilers looked like an impossible challenge, a team that could win it all indefinitely. The knowledge weighed heavily on McDonald. Of all the NHL players who've worn championship rings over the years, no one ever wanted one more than McDonald. Through all the close calls and the years he spent out of the playoffs, McDonald never lost sight of that teen-age dream.

"The thing about Lanny," says his wife Ardell, "is that he never lost his enthusiasm. Just before Lanny was drafted, he and a friend of his and I went to see *Face Off*, the movie that was supposed to be about Jim McKenny. They just sat there watching with stars in their eyes, thinking 'So that's what the NHL is all about.' Lanny's never lost that feeling, that 'Wow, this is the NHL.'"

Heading into the spring of '86, McDonald's niggling injuries gradually disappeared. In March, McDonald discarded the cumbersome knee brace he wore in favour of a smaller, lighter brace that gave him more mobility. Moreover, he discovered why his shot — the most important weapon in his scoring arsenal — was betraying him in the latter half of the season. Instead of snapping his shot, McDonald's trademark over the years, he was fanning on it or getting it away with little pace or speed. The change was obvious to everyone, including goaltender Reggie Lemelin, McDonald's roommate and a player who had faced his shot in practice every day during his sixty-six goal season. The two went through all the possibilities and finally hit on it. McDonald's sticks were wrong. The lie — the angle of the blade in relationship to the shaft — was a few degrees out. The difference would hardly matter to a beer leaguer, but it meant a great deal to McDonald.

So McDonald brought down an autographed stick from his 1984 collection and compared it to his current sticks. They were two lies apart. That meant McDonald was shooting everything farther away from his body than he liked or was used to. Under normal circumstances, McDonald liked to drag the puck along and shoot it when it was almost in his feet. The incorrect lie brought the heel of the blade off the ice when he was shooting. As a result, he was mishandling the puck.

Adjusting the sticks provided an immediate benefit. McDonald ended the season with a flourish, scoring six goals in nine games to finish the year with twenty-eight, a respectable total considering the balance the Flames' scoring eventually developed. In addition, he had played in all eighty games. Only rookie Gary Suter matched that achievement. McDonald predicted he could overcome the knee and abdomen injuries that hindered him the past two seasons and play every game and he did. "Not bad for a youngster, eh?" said McDonald, understandably proud of his achievement. "I think there were a lot of questions in everybody's mind before the season started. I guess maybe I answered them."

When the Flames filed onto the ice for the first playoff series against the Winnipeg Jets, Johnson decided to use a line that he had experimented with off and on. Risebrough centred McDonald and Tonelli. Together, the trio became known as the not-ready-for-retirement players. The nickname stuck. It had to. McDonald was playing like the McDonald of old, not like an old McDonald.

Johnson reasoned that McDonald needed a centre that would complement his game. "He's not a European player," said Johnson. "He doesn't change from wing to wing. He doesn't regroup the way Hakan Loob does. When you see Lanny, he's always coming down the right side. He needs an old-time centre to play with him.''

McDonald and his linemates put it together right away against the Jets. In overtime of the third game, McDonald took a pass from Tonelli, wound up and put the winner past rookie goaltender Daniel Berthiaume, the fourth goaltender used by the Jets in the series. Earlier, Brian Hayward, Dan Bouchard, and Marc Behrend had all received the call. No one could keep the old-timers off the scoresheet. When the series ended, the trio were the team's leading scorers.

Against the Oilers, McDonald's experience perhaps more than anything helped the team pick itself up from each of its three losses to win the next game. When the Flames finally brought the St. Louis Blues to their knees in seven tense games, it appeared as if everybody around the NHL was cheering for McDonald. As the Flames and Blues shook hands following the last game, even St. Louis coach Jacques Demers pulled McDonald aside and wished him well.

''I coached Paul Baxter,'' said Demers. ''I coached Joey Mullen and Terry Johnson. For their sakes, I hope they all win. But the one guy I really hope can put a Stanley Cup ring on his finger is Lanny McDonald. He is such a great inspiration to youngsters. He has represented the hockey world with such class over the years and it reflects on that hockey club. Nothing against Montreal, but I wish him the best in the final. I admire the man. You hear all these things in the world about drugs and athletes, but Lanny McDonald is above that. He stands the tallest of all.''

The win over St. Louis put McDonald into the first Stanley Cup final of his distinguished twelve-year career. The only other time he'd qualified for the Stanley Cup semifinals, the Maple Leafs lost the series to the Montreal Canadiens in four consecutive games. That was in 1978. Now, a full eight years later, McDonald found himself in uncharted waters.

"I don't think this team is going to stop," said McDonald. "I'm not just saying that because I don't want it to stop. I'd say in preparation, in talent, in work ethic, we are in good shape. Plus, we've come too far to throw in the towel. It's too important to us. Not just to the old guys, but to the young guys, too. More and more, everybody's realizing that there aren't that many chances out there to win it all. The boys are really afraid of letting the guy beside him down, so they're not doing it. It's a good feeling when your hockey club gets to that stage. It doesn't happen all the time. You can be close talent-wise, but sometimes the little ingredients are missing. This club has a little bit of all the things it takes to win."

4
The "So-called" Slump

"We're in a slump because people keep telling us we're in a slump." BOB JOHNSON

Just in case the memory of the previous year's playoff disaster slipped anybody's mind over the summer, general manager Cliff Fletcher's preparations for the 1985 season were designed to act as a gentle reminder. Their first-round loss to the Winnipeg Jets earned fifty-nine players and two coaching staffs an all-expenses paid trip to Moncton, N.B., home of the team's No. 1 minor-league affiliate, the Golden Flames. It gave the players a chance to sample the lobster, dine with the Charles Bourgeoises, and get their minds on hockey right away — without the distractions of family, friends, and casual acquaintances who wanted to know what had happened against the Jets.

Coming off their most successful regular season ever, the Flames' management faced something of a dilemma. The team was a solid fifth overall the year before, an excellent result. They achieved their primary goal — reducing the gap between themselves and the Oilers — but they failed to foresee that the Jets would improve even more, leapfrog past them into second place in the Smythe Division, and then knock them out of the playoffs five days into the post-season tournament.

Accordingly, the Flames had retooled their line-up, dumping five players who were regulars one year ago: Kent Nilsson, Kari Eloranta, Don Edwards, Steve Tambellini, and Jim Jackson. Nilsson and Edwards were traded. Eloranta, Tambellini, and Jackson were released. The idea was to give up some scoring to improve defensively. Nilsson scored ninety-nine points in his final year with Calgary, good for seventeenth in the league. No other player broke into the top forty-five. Without Nilsson, the Flames were a much-improved team defensively. But who would score the goals?

Everybody, answered coach Bob Johnson. Borrowing a page from the St. Louis Cardinals' bullpen-by-committee, the Flames introduced a plan for scoring-by-committee. No single player needed to score fifty goals if half-a-dozen players could score thirty. The Flames set out to play generic hockey, trying to Brand-X opponents to death. It may have lacked the box office appeal that Edmonton's wide-open style held, but it was their only choice to be competitive.

The absence of finesse players such as Nilsson, Eloranta, and Tambellini also changed the team's character. If the Smythe Division was an unpopularity contest, then the Flames would win it hands down. The Flames were returning to a tradition established in Atlanta, by adding muscle to their line-up. More and more, they became the team nobody wanted to play against. The new-look Flames were to play the grinding style associated with the old Boston Bruins teams. Knowing they couldn't match the Oilers stride for stride, the Flames introduced a new blueprint. Instead of trying to keep up with their opponents, the Flames wanted to slow them down and maybe wear them down.

They could afford to play that style because the one edge

they held over every other team in the NHL, including the Oilers, was their extraordinary depth. Including the games missed by left winger Dave Hindmarch, who retired on the eve of training camp, the Flames lost 357 man-games to injuries the year before. As a result, they were able to develop a depth chart that was unprecedented around the NHL. Johnson opened training camp with fifteen forwards or five complete forward lines, all of whom finished the season in Calgary. Johnson had put a game-breaking player, someone along the lines of a Mike Bossy or a Tim Kerr, on the top of his off-season shopping list. Players of that calibre rarely come available and when they do, an asterisk is too often attached to their names. Fletcher failed to deal for a game-breaker, leaving Johnson to either develop his own or do without.

The Flames began the year by doing without. Johnson thought the team's success would hinge on consistency. Not much separated the team's first line from its fourth line. From game to game, one was hard-pressed to tell the difference between lines. On opening day, Calgary succeeded both in beating and in beating up on the Winnipeg Jets. The Flames' 8-3 win in a game marred by a rare bench-clearing incident didn't make up for the team's loss in the 1985 playoffs, but it established a pattern for the season. Before the game started, the players downplayed the rivalry that the playoff meeting began. They said there was no lasting bitterness, no talk of vendettas, nothing but a new start on a clean slate.

But all the good intentions evaporated when fight night broke out in the second period. Jets' goaltender Brian Hayward speared Flames' right winger Tim Hunter after Hunter encroached on this territory by charging into the crease. Hayward earned an automatic game misconduct for the spear. The teams milled about innocently enough until Hunter freed himself from the linesman and found himself facing Jets' defenceman Dave Ellett. Hunter evaded Ellett and continued to spar with Hayward. When he started to get the upper hand, the Jets, led by defenceman Tim Watters, charged off the bench. The Flames were right behind them. As the melee started to run its course, Hunter found himself by the Jets' bench where assistant coach Rick Bowness swung at him from the bench. That earned Bowness a disqualification, too. When the ice chips settled, five players and one coach had been ejected, 122 minutes in penalties had been assessed, and play in the second period had been suspended. When the teams returned for a third period that lasted twenty-six minutes and eleven seconds, the Flames made short work of Hayward's replacement in the Jets' goal, Marc Behrend. They scored five times to win going away. Perry Berezan scored two, while six players chipped in with single goals.

The Flames were on their way. Scoring by committee was working. So was the physical, bruising style that they adopted. Around the Smythe Division, every coach — Edmonton's Glen Sather, Vancouver's Tom Watt, Winnipeg's Barry Long, and Los Angeles's Pat Quinn — complained about the Flames' approach to the game. In Calgary, no one listened. By December 1, the Flames were winning with such ridiculous consistency that it was almost becoming dull. They won with balanced scoring, they won with better defence, and they won with excellent goaltending from Reggie Lemelin. On the last day of November, their 4-3 win over the New York Islanders gave them an 8-2-3 record for the month, their most successful November in team history. By mid-December, for one night they were tied for third overall with the Washington Capitals.

Then it happened. No one knew exactly how it started nor how long it would last, but from the 14th of December to the 7th of January, the Flames — completely, utterly, resolutely —

collapsed. Ironically, some of the trouble could be traced to the team's success and the way they achieved it. With twenty-four players on the major-league roster, Johnson was rotating players in and out all the time. Problem was, the Flames were winning no matter who played. As a result, when the team's depth forced up to four contributing players to sit out every night, the discontent began to grow. The players were asking themselves why they weren't playing if their play was adequate and the team continued to win.

Steve Bozek had been on both sides of the fence. In his first two years in Calgary, Bozek was a part-time player, someone Johnson referred to as a role player. If the team was healthy, invariably Bozek would be the odd man out. Designated sitters became known as the designated Bozek. This year, however, Bozek was playing exceptionally well and Johnson couldn't bring himself to rotate him out of the lineup. Bozek saw it coming: ''The coaches say they like the extra players,'' he said one day, ''but it makes their job harder. Who can you point the finger at? Let's face it. Nobody's played that badly. Everybody's playing pretty well.''

Ultimately, Johnson failed to keep the peace. His reaction to the player grumbling was to get tough. That was out of character and it didn't work. ''Do they want to go to Moncton?'' Johnson asked rhetorically. ''We could always send a couple of players to Moncton. Oh, I know all the guys want to play, but our job is to have a winning team. We're trying to turn the competition into a positive thing. The guys who aren't playing can use the time to work on their off-ice conditioning and really push the people who are in the line-up.''

Johnson's point worked better in theory than in practice. The grumbling continued and it became a distraction. Suddenly, everything became just a little off centre, a little out of kilter. The slide had started. When it hit, it hit hard.

The first loss came innocently enough. The Flames, who were 7-1 in their previous eight games, went to Vancouver to play the Canucks, who had lost twelve of their last fourteen. The Canucks, sinking fast in the Smythe Division, needed a lifeline and the Flames tossed them one. Goaltender Reggie Lemelin allowed three first-period goals, causing Johnson to replace him with Marc D'Amour for the start of the second period. The Flames fought back far enough to tie it, then lost the game when Thomas Gradin scored late to give the Canucks a 4-3 win.

The second loss came on a thoroughly forgettable night in Pittsburgh when Lemelin failed to go the distance for the second game in a row. This time, they fell behind 4-0, mounted a furious, second-half comeback, and once again came up a goal short.

The inconsistent play of their special teams cost them the third loss. On a night in which right winger Tim Hunter couldn't stay out of the penalty box, Hartford Whalers scored three times with the man advantage to win 4-3, Calgary's third consecutive loss by the same score. Once again, the Flames held an edge territorially, but couldn't get the tying goal on Whalers' goaltender Steve Weeks.

The Flames' missing-in-action power-play contributed to their fourth consecutive defeat, a 5-2 loss to the St. Louis Blues, — their longest losing streak of that season, last season, or any season since February, 1982. In the first thirty minutes, the Flames received five power-play chances, including one fifty-seven second span in which the Blues played two men short, but they couldn't score even a single goal with the man advantage. The Blues snapped a scoreless tie late in the second period with three fast goals and won going away.

In the final game before the Christmas break, two Alberta-born, Edmonton-raised grinches named Troy Murray and Ken

Yaremchuk cast a pall over the Flames' holiday plans when they helped rally the Chicago Black Hawks to a 5-4 win, Calgary's fifth consecutive loss. Needing a win to right the wrongs of the past ten days, the Flames ran into some familiar stumbling blocks: good goaltending, poor finish around the goal, and some unlucky bounces. They had enough chances to win five games, which is exactly how many they didn't win on the road trip. ''I don't think I've ever gone through a five-game slump with a team when we really hadn't played that badly,'' said right winger Lanny McDonald, and his words echoed through the dressing room as the team split up for the three-day break.

If the Flames thought the holiday would put them back on track, they were in for a disappointment. Back in Calgary, two days after Christmas, the Flames suffered the strangest loss of all. Falling behind 4-0 to the Philadelphia Flyers, the Flames rallied to tie the game 4-4, then lost it when the Flyers' Rich Sutter accidently caromed a centring pass out of the corner, off of two skates and behind Lemelin.

As if they didn't have enough to worry about, the Flames were scheduled to play an exhibition game against a touring Soviet team, the Moscow Dynamo, the next night. Moscow won every game but one on its tour. The next night the Flames temporarily ended their losing ways with a 3-2 win over the Russian team. Mike Vernon, up from the minors because of a slight groin injury to Marc D'Amour, picked up the win in goal, his first ever in a Flames' uniform. Knocking off the Russians gave the team a badly needed boost of confidence, but it didn't help Vernon or Gino Cavallini or Neil Sheehy. On New Year's Day, the Flames demoted all three to Moncton, reducing their roster from twenty-four to twenty-one players. ''As soon as we got everybody healthy, we started having problems,'' said Fletcher. ''We had a lot of players and a lot of anxiety about who was and who wasn't playing. So we decided to send them down. They'll be back.''

The next day, the Flames reverted to their play of the past fortnight, dropping a 6-3 decision to the Minnesota North Stars, their seventh consecutive loss in league play. Even Willi Plett, the ex-Flames' player who had seen his share of bad teams, couldn't believe how far they'd fallen. "Like everything else, winning is a habit and losing is a habit," said Plett. Clearly, he implied, the Flames were addicted to losing.

Things didn't look much brighter either. Just when they needed a break from the schedule-maker, the Flames looked up and saw they were playing the Edmonton Oilers in two of the next three games. The Oilers made it eight losses in a row for the Flames by scoring a 4-3 win that wasn't as close as the score suggested. Really, the game was only close in the last minute when Gary Suter's second goal of the game with D'Amour on the bench for a sixth attacker brought them to within one. Not since 1974, when Bernie Geoffrion was coaching them in Atlanta, had the Flames lost eight games in a row.

Two nights later, a 6-5 loss to the Montreal Canadiens established a franchise record for futility — nine consecutive losses. It was the seventh by a single goal. It could have gone either way. It just didn't.

Calgary made it an imperfect ten against the Oilers in Edmonton where the Flames almost never win. Their 6-3 defeat dropped them below .500 for the first time since October 26. Their starting goaltender didn't finish the game — for the third game in a row. Their special teams were below par. Johnson thought he saw "flashes" of their earlier form, but maybe it was just the lights of the interrogation room where he was trying — and not succeeding — to explain the team's slump. Johnson wouldn't even acknowledge that ten

51

consecutive losses constituted a slump. Trying to keep his poise as everybody around him lost theirs, Johnson commented: ''You say to yourself, let's go back to the time when we were successful. What did we do differently? For the six weeks when we lost only two games, we were getting some breaks, we were getting some timely goals, and our goaltending was outstanding. Now, all of a sudden, we're not getting many goals, our defence is too tentative, and we're not getting good goaltending. We're in a slump because people keep telling us we're in a slump. People tell you you're playing badly and after a while, you start to believe it. People tell you you're playing great and you believe that, too. What do we need? We need to recapture the winning feeling. And the only way to do that is to win a game.''

The effects of Johnson's optimistic words lasted less than a day. The Hartford Whalers paid a visit to the Olympic Saddledome and buried the Flames 9-1. Even Johnson couldn't find a silver lining in the decisive loss. ''It was our worst performance in the four years I've been here,'' he said. ''We had absolutely nothing going for us. People keep telling the players and they keep reading that they're in a slump and all of a sudden, they feel sorry for themselves. Usually, as a coach, you try to find the positive aspects of a game. Tonight, there were no positive aspects. None. Period. We have absolutely no excuses. All we want now are solutions. And we'll find solutions.''

Playing against a Whalers' team that came into the game with three consecutive losses, the Flames looked as if they'd struggled against a midget team. Their eleventh consecutive loss carved them an unwelcome niche in the NHL record book. It gave them a share of the eighth longest losing streak ever. The Washington Capitals once lost seventeen in a row. The Philadelphia Quakers once lost fifteen in a row. Two teams lost fourteen in a row, three lost twelve in a row. Then came the

Calgary Flames, 1985-86.

Did the Flames quit against the Whalers, trying to engineer changes? Even the suggestion caused some players to bristle. Said McDonald: "The guys didn't quit. Unfortunately, when it gets to a stage like this, the guys don't react as quickly as they should. Things went constantly downhill from start to finish. I look at this as a time when everybody hit rock bottom, when we got our butts kicked and got them kicked good. I don't have the answers. The only thing we can do is come out for the next game and work hard."

Fletcher promised changes following the loss to the Whalers, but when they came, they were hardly startling. Vernon returned from Moncton accompanied by Sheehy and rookie Mark Lamb. All three were in the lineup when the Canucks — the team that started all of this misery — paid a visit to the Saddledome. The Flames played the game as if they were on tenterhooks. When regulation play ended, the teams were tied 4-4. In the first minute of overtime, Jim Peplinski took a pass from Perry Berezan, shot low inside the post, and put it past Wendell Young to give the Flames a 5-4 win.

Officially, that ended the streak — but not the troubles. During the slump, the Flames slipped from third to thirteenth overall. Their power play dropped from third to nineteenth overall. More importantly, the level of the Flames' play dropped off dramatically. They played much better in the first five losses than they did when they finally defeated the Canucks. No one could really say they were back. That took time. The Flames took advantage of a lull in the schedule, staggering to wins in three of the next five games, including decisions over the Detroit Red Wings and the Toronto Maple Leafs, the twenty-first and twentieth-place teams in the league. The de facto turnaround would have to wait for February, when the changes finally came. The slump was over. But not forgotten.

5
The Trading Game

"Maybe I shouldn't be saying this, but trading a player
like Kent Nilsson never hurts you."

WILLI PLETT, MINNESOTA NORTH STARS

Trader Cliff, they used to call him. For Christmas in 1983, the
Calgary Flames' staff came up with the perfect gift for their
boss, general manager Cliff Fletcher: a framed picture of television game show host Monty Hall. In autographing his photo,
Hall wrote: "To Cliff Fletcher, the only man who makes more
deals than I do."

It was an inside story. In Fletcher's first three seasons in
Calgary, he had made twenty separate trades involving players
on the Flames' major-league roster. Not even Minnesota's
Lou Nanne could keep pace with him. As Fletcher made trade
after trade, trying to dispose of all the old Atlanta Flames'
players who wanted out of Calgary, he became known as the
NHL's answer to Monty Hall, the man ready to trade a former
No. 1 draft choice for whatever you had behind door No. 2.

Then, inexplicably, it all stopped. When the general
managers sat down to deal, Fletcher would disappear. He
couldn't be found. From July 5th, 1983 until May 30, 1985,
Fletcher did not add a single player to his team via the trade

route. The only transaction he made was to dump centre Guy Chouinard for his salary to the St. Louis Blues. Fletcher wanted his younger players to develop before he turned to the most difficult part of building a team — fine tuning a contender into a champion.

The 1984-85 season had opened his eyes. A funny thing happened on the way to a playoff series with the Edmonton Oilers. The Flames never got there. They had lost hard and fast to the Winnipeg Jets. Something that looked so good at the end of the regular season disappeared from the Stanley Cup playoff in five days. Something went wrong. Someone had to be blamed. That someone turned out to be Kent Nilsson, the highest scoring player in the history of the franchise.

Controversy followed Nilsson around wherever he went, even if he personally wanted little to do with it. He was loved and hated in Calgary. When the Flames won, he was the reason. When they lost, he was to blame. There was no middle ground in the fans' relationship with Nilsson. Win, lose, or tie, he was the player people left talking about. Nilsson mirrored almost exactly the ups and downs of the franchise. In hockey circles, the Flames were thought of as a team with talent that didn't play up to expectations. Nilsson was viewed the same way. When Calgary lost to Winnipeg in April of 1985, it was clear that Nilsson's tour of duty with the Flames was over. The problem was, everyone in hockey knew it.

On the day after the season ended, Fletcher made it clear Nilsson was not an untouchable. This represented a change in club philosophy. In the past, the Flames accepted Nilsson for what he was: a talented, if erratic player who could not be depended upon when the playoff race began. The thinking was that Nilsson could be part of a Stanley Cup winner, but not necessarily the catalyst.

"The question we asked ourselves and I asked every

hockey person in the organization was: are we a better team with or without Kent Nilsson?'' Fletcher said. He never did answer his own question publicly. His silence was answer enough. Word of Nilsson's availability circulated in the hockey world, but few offers came Fletcher's way. The ones that did were ridiculously low. In the weeks that followed, one thing became apparent. The almost uncoachable Nilsson was almost untradeable. The Flames couldn't trade him to Pittsburgh for centre Mike Bullard. They couldn't trade him to the Rangers for injury-prone defenceman Barry Beck. Montreal Canadiens, a team that needed scoring, wouldn't part with steady defence-man Craig Ludwig for Nilsson. Nilsson had the ultimate in double-edged nicknames and it hindered Fletcher's attempts to trade him. He was called the Magic Man: originally for his brilliance with the puck, later for his ability to disappear in close games. Running out of places to look, Fletcher eventually turned to Nanne, his close friend. They had done business before. On Saturday, June 15, 1986, they did business again. Minutes before the annual NHL entry draft in Toronto, Nilsson and a third-round draft choice had been traded to the Minnesota North Stars for two second-round picks. It looked like a fire sale. Even Nilsson's detractors couldn't believe how little he commanded in the NHL trade market. People asked: How could the Flames have given Nilsson away? Had Fletcher blown it?

But the Flames did what they had set out to do. They added by subtracting. They improved the club by removing one of its troubled parts. Earlier that summer, Fletcher had made a similar move, sending goaltender Don Edwards to the Toronto Maple Leafs. Again, no other player was involved in the exchange. Fletcher stood firm in his belief that he'd done the right thing. One year later, when the Flames advanced to the Stanley Cup final, few people remembered Kent Nilsson.

With Nilsson gone and coach Bob Johnson clamouring

for a quality goal scorer, Fletcher set a second plan in action later in the summer. The St. Louis Blues were having trouble signing Joey Mullen, the American-born right winger, who had averaged forty goals per season the last two years. Mullen's agent Larry Rauch and St. Louis owner Harry Ornest took almost all summer to come up with a new contract for the free-agent winger. The Flames couldn't afford to risk signing Mullen themselves because the compensation that he would command was more than what they were prepared to surrender. So Fletcher opened trade talks in August with his Blues' counterpart, Ron Caron.

Caron had always liked Eddy Beers. He saw Beers as a high-scoring, relatively tough winger who could play on a line with Bernie Federko and Mark Hunter. Names were dropped back and forth, mostly by Caron. The Flames wanted to deal Beers for Mullen. The Blues wanted Beers and centre Carey Wilson for Mullen. No deal. When the Flames said they wouldn't trade Wilson, Caron switched tactics. He asked for defenceman Allan MacInnis and Beers for Mullen. Still no deal. Caron didn't stop there. He then asked for Beers and draft pick Joe Nieuwendyk, ironically one of the picks the Flames had received in the Nilsson trade, for Mullen. The bartering went on all through the summer. By the time the season began, the Mullen deal looked dead. Neither side would give and Mullen, frustrated, signed a one-year contract for the same money he'd been offered all along. For better or worse, he was married to St. Louis for another year. Or so he thought.

Until the Flames were well into their eleven game losing streak, there was little reason for Fletcher to make a deal. Suddenly, the questions came. Suddenly, Kent Nilsson's name was being bandied about again. This never would have happened if Nilsson was still here, fans said on John Henderson's open-line phone-in show. The pressure was on Fletcher and on coach

Bob Johnson. Who would be the first to be traded? Who would be the first to be fired? How would this club be turned around?

Throughout the eleven game losing streak much was said but little was accomplished. Something was supposed to happen. But it didn't. Even when Fletcher was asked if the Flames were still interested in Mullen, the question was followed by a denial. The denial should have been the tip-off. On the first day of February, following a 4-4 tie against the Edmonton Oilers at the Olympic Saddledome, the Flames scheduled a news conference. Standing at the back of the press room, Oilers' assistant coaches John Muckler and Bob McCammon watched as Fletcher announced his deal. The deal would push the Flames one step closer to the Stanley Cup champions. That night, the Flames had acquired Mullen and defencemen Terry Johnson and Rik Wilson for Beers, winger Gino Cavallini, and defenceman Charles Bourgeois.

In Mullen, the Flames got what they wanted. A genuine goal scorer. In Beers, Cavallini, and Bourgeois, the Blues had added depth to a lineup that needed it. Johnson became an extra defenceman in the Flames' scheme of things. Wilson, a throw-in, was traded to the Chicago Black Hawks for a minor-leaguer who was subsequently released. Mullen was the prize. Always known as a goal scorer, the Blues were prepared to surrender him because they thought he was too slow. That he wanted too much money. That he wasn't a playoff scorer. "It's a funny thing," Mullen said, upon hearing the stories. "I didn't hear anything about these problems until I got to Calgary. I guess you don't hear those things until after you're gone. But to be honest, I'm not doing anything differently than I've done before." Mullen, listed inaccurately in the statistics sheets as 5 feet 8 inches, 180 pounds, was indeed smaller than that. Other than by playing him, there was no real way to measure his heart. The Flames found out fast that

58

Mullen may have been small, but he was also tough. Even if he wasn't the fastest skater in hockey, he would usually get there, which is all the Flames asked of him. His contract, which had caused him so much trouble in St. Louis, was quickly re-negotiated when he joined the Flames. His future was secured in a long-term million-dollar deal. The question of his ability to score in the playoffs was quickly answered in his first five post-season games. He scored six goals.

Mullen didn't take long to make a favourable impression on the Flames. By adding Mullen, the Flames had strengthened the right wing considerably. Along with Hakan Loob, Lanny McDonald and big Tim Hunter, they had as good a right side as any team in the league. It was equally clear how anemic the left side was in comparison. Fletcher knew it. Bob Johnson knew it. They needed more help before they could seriously challenge the Oilers. Fletcher decided he wanted left winger John Ogrodnick from the Detroit Red Wings, and he thought he was going to get him.

Just as Fletcher and Caron negotiated back and forth trying to complete the Mullen deal, so too did Fletcher and Detroit general manager Jimmy Devellano discuss Ogrodnick. Devellano had been having all kinds of problems in Detroit. His club was in last place. He had already fired coach Harry Neale and replaced him with the inexperienced Brad Park. And Park, who had been given a fancy title, was quietly warring with Devellano over control of the Red Wings. With all this going on, the Flames attempted to make a deal for Ogrodnick, the fifty goal scorer with the powerful shot off the left wing. For weeks, names were dropped back and forth. The Flames wanted Ogrodnick as much as the Red Wings wanted to trade him. Ogrodnick didn't say much himself, but let it be known that he thought his career in Detroit was over.

The longer Fletcher and Devellano spoke, the more

complicated the offers became. Devellano was looking to make changes, serious changes, which meant for multi-player offers. At one time, there had been talk of a six-for-five swap, which would have sent Jim Peplinski, Dan Quinn, Al MacInnis, Richard Kromm, Colin Patterson, and Eddy Beers to Detroit for Ogrodnick, Ron Duguay, Reed Larson, Kelly Kisio, and Greg Smith. Ironically, the Flames would eventually trade Beers and Kromm. The Red Wings would eventually trade all players proposed, except Ogrodnick. The deal, as it was proposed, was laughable from a Flames' perspective. They didn't want to trade the nucleus of an above-average team for the nucleus of the worst team in the league. But Fletcher had proven his ability to wait at the trade tables. Talks stalled and eventually broke off just days before the March 11th trading deadline.

Unable to trade for Ogrodnick, the Flames looked elsewhere for help. First, they talked to the Toronto Maple Leafs about acquiring disgruntled captain Rick Vaive. If they could have acquired Vaive, they were prepared to turn around and send him to Detroit for Ogrodnick. Had that not worked out, they would have kept Vaive on the right side and moved Hakan Loob to left wing.

Meanwhile, the rumours out of Quebec had begun. The Nordiques were having problems of their own, and they were shopping around for a defenceman. The name they were shopping sounded attractive: Michel Goulet, the talented fifty goal scorer who had come under question in Quebec. The Nordiques were interested in Steve Konroyd and Al MacInnis, but they weren't necessarily prepared to give up Goulet. The Nordiques were more interested in moving John Anderson, the former Maple Leaf with the biggest moustache this side of McDonald's. The Flames talked to the Nordiques. The Flames were intrigued by the possibility of adding Goulet, but the price in any transaction would be too high. Jim Peplinski, for one. Konroyd or MacInnis, for another. And likely something else. Again, a deal couldn't be worked out. Quebec wound up trading Anderson to Hartford for Risto Siltanen. So as the trading deadline approached, the Flames were once again shopping around for a trade, unsure of where to turn next.

The day before the deadline, a most unlikely option came up. Another friend of Fletcher's, Bill Torrey of the New York Islanders, had called and he was dangling an interesting player: John Tonelli. All-star left winger John Tonelli. Not a scorer, but a mucker. Canada Cup Most Valuable Player, Tonelli. Four-time Stanley Cup champion. That John Tonelli. Fletcher almost dropped the phone.

Tonelli, who played such a big part on the Islander championship teams, had fallen from favour on Long Island. His season had begun in a contract dispute and it didn't get better as the year went along. Mid-way through the season, the Islanders brought talent evaluator Gerry Ehman along on a road trip in an attempt to understand why the Islanders weren't playing well. Islander coach Al Arbour asked Ehman what he thought of Tonelli after a game in Winnipeg. Ehman's comments were not favourable. The next game, against the North Stars in Minnesota, Tonelli was benched for the first time as an Islander. Things were never the same between Tonelli and Arbour again. As the deadline approached, Fletcher and Torrey moved fast. Calgary needed a winger. The Islanders needed a defenceman. When the trade was finally made, hours before dealing was to be suspended for another season, the Flames had acquired Tonelli for defenceman Steve Konroyd and forward Richard Kromm. Fletcher had used the George Allen approach in trading for the aging Tonelli. The future was now for the Flames. He knew it. He had given up a part of the future in Konroyd and Kromm. If the Flames' acquisition of Mullen smacked of the on-going struggle to catch the Oilers, the second deal confirmed it. The Flames were ecstatic with their deal. So were the Islanders. Everyone was ecstatic. Everyone except John Tonelli. Upon hearing news of the deal, Tonelli stormed out of the Nassau Coliseum and went for a drive. He kept to himself most of that day, trying to control his emotions. He couldn't. He wasn't happy on the Island, and he wasn't happy to be traded. He was mad at Al Arbour for misusing him and he was mad at Torrey for trading him. His mind scrambled to control his thoughts, but it would take days before Tonelli would have it all in perspective.

What made things especially difficult for Tonelli were the circumstances of the trade. That night, the Flames, his new team, were playing the Islanders, his old team. Tonelli arrived at the Nassau County Coliseum about 4:30 and was immediately collared for a television interview. He pulled on Tim Hunter's sweater and politely answered the questions. Then he brushed off the remaining reporters, saying he had a game to prepare for. After the Islanders recorded a one-sided victory, Tonelli was the last player out of the shower, trying to postpone the inevitable confrontation with the New York press. He spent much of the post-game explaining his feelings to those he had known for years. What he didn't know that night was he would soon get an opportunity to play for the Stanley Cup again. With the Flames.

While it took Tonelli time to overcome his shock, the trade itself sent shockwaves through the NHL. In Minnesota, where the Oilers were preparing for a game against the North Stars, Glen Sather was upset that the Flames had acquired Tonelli. Sather said he didn't know Tonelli was available. He then accused Torrey of trying to help his old pal Fletcher knock off the Oilers. Torrey would have been happy to see anyone knock off the Oilers, the team that ended the Islanders' dynasty. But he wouldn't do it at his own expense. Still, the Tonelli trade bothered the Oilers. Especially the defencemen who would have to deal with the wrath of Tonelli in the corners. "I'm not looking ahead to playing the Oilers," Tonelli said a few days after the trade. And the Oilers weren't looking forward to playing the Flames.

In acquiring Tonelli and Mullen, the Flames had shown a quality which they had sometimes previously lacked in dealing: timing. They had made the right moves at the right time. They had added ability and character to a team in need of both. Quickly, Mullen fit in on a line with rookie centre Joel Otto and co-captain Jim Peplinski. The transition took Tonelli longer. Eventually, he found his way to a line of his peers. He played with McDonald and Doug Risebrough — the not-ready-for-retirement players. They played over their heads and below their ages. The line became the heart of the Flames.

Quietly, one move was overlooked on the day the Flames acquired Tonelli. They had also made another deal for a minor-league forward who hadn't played a game in four months. On paper, the Flames may have been no closer to beating the Oilers with Tonelli and Mullen, but with the addition of Nick Fotiu, they were closer to beating them up. Fotiu wasted little time in becoming a Calgary favourite. For starters, he didn't wear a helmet, which meant for instant recognition. Not only did Fotiu bring his roller-derby style of play from the New York Rangers, he also brought an old custom: puck throwing. Before every game, Fotiu would skate around the ice, tossing pucks to fans searching for souvenirs, often testing his arm by heaving pucks to the highest levels of the Saddledome. Fotiu was a rogue, a throw-back, a tough-guy on skates, who could skate fast but do little else than entertain. The Oilers had Dave Semenko and Don Jackson and Marty McSorley, all of whom are better known for fistic prowess than ability to score goals.

These men score with their fists. Lefts and rights, with some-one counting at the knockdowns. Fotiu's addition to the Flames meant the tag-team matches could officially begin.

Unlike Tonelli, who grew up in the hockey hotbed of southern Ontario, Mullen and Fotiu came from less likely surroundings. As a kid, Fotiu would carry a hatchet in his hockey bag when he rode the New York subways from Coney Island to middle-of-the-night practice sessions in New York. He never actually used the hatchet. He threatened to use it once. Mullen grew up in a world of hatchets: Clinton, New York, otherwise known as Hell's Kitchen.

Mullen learned to play hockey on roller skates before transforming his skills to ice. He learned about the game from his father, who was a maintenance man at Madison Square Garden. Later Mullen would go back as the highest scorer from the New York area. Oddly enough, he was playing for a Canadian team.

Mullen, Tonelli, and Fotiu all added something to the Flames. Mullen's contribution came in goals and assists. Tonelli's contribution was not as easy to measure. How much did his efforts inspire others? How much did his raging-bull style make his linemates play harder? Fotiu's contribution came mostly off the ice. He combined with Jim Peplinski to keep the team loose. If one wasn't playing a practical joke, the other was. Peplinski received the blame because his teammates knew his style. Fotiu was a newcomer. In the end, each of them made a difference. In his own way.

6
The Unlikely Finalists

"What we really need is more Risebroughs."

BOB JOHNSON

It was the spring of 1982 and the Montreal Canadiens had hit one of those slow periods, the kind that were supposed to affect everybody in hockey but them. The once peerless Habs had drifted into the middle of the NHL pack, a position normally reserved for teams with other names from other places. Something had gone wrong with hockey's greatest franchise: the Canadiens had stopped winning championships. With Ken Dryden and Guy Lafleur and Serge Savard and Guy Lapointe in the line-up, they had won four in a row from 1975 to 1979. Then something went wrong. Three years had passed since they'd last won. Three years of early playoff exits, three years of fans screaming for changes, was forcing them to act. Lafleur remained, but Dryden had retired and Savard and Lapointe were on their way out. Scotty Bowman, the successful coach, had left Montreal for Buffalo years before. Sam Pollock, the genius general manager, had left hockey for private business, leaving Irving Grundman in charge of the troubled Canadiens. Grundman needed to wheel and deal, if only to prove that he was trying to put the Canadiens back on track. In the end, Grundman's moves would directly affect the course three clubs, including Calgary, would take.

On September 9, 1982, Rod Langway and his tax troubles were traded to the Washington Capitals, turning that struggling franchise around overnight. The Canadiens took Ryan Walter and Rick Green in exchange for Langway and three others. It took them almost four years to reap any benefit from the deal. The same day as Langway headed to Washington, the Flames made an apparently incidental deal, also with the Canadiens. They, like the Capitals, have never been the same since.

Doug Risebrough was riding the stationary exercise bicycle in the Canadiens' workout room when he heard the news. The reaction of a traded player rarely differs. First, they want to know where. Then, they want to know for whom. Sometimes, they want to know why. Risebrough already knew why. He had asked Grundman to deal him — if management decided he wasn't part of the team's plans. He heard Calgary and he was pleased. He heard that he was traded for two draft picks, and didn't know what to think. Every player would like to think he's worth more. Risebrough continued to pedal, completed his workout, said his goodbyes, and packed his bags, Two days later, he had reported to the Flames' training camp.

The hockey world was so stunned by the dimensions of the Langway deal, few even bothered to notice the Risebrough trade. That group did not include Edmonton boss Glen Sather, who had previously tried to pry his old teammate loose from the Canadiens. The Oilers needed Risebrough. Not only did they need help at centre, they needed leadership help. Sather made an offer for Risebrough, but was turned down. The Canadiens wanted nothing to do with the Oilers, having lost to them in a recent playoff series. Flames' general manager Cliff Fletcher, who had maintained strong relationships with the Canadiens after a decade of working there, made the deal instead. But even Fletcher, years later, would admit one thing. When he made the trade on September 9, 1982, he didn't know how big a deal it really was.

Some thought at the time that the Flames didn't need Risebrough. He was a small centre, they said, who didn't score, was always injured, and had seen his better days. The Flames already had character players in Lanny McDonald and Mel Bridgman. They had Kent Nilsson and Guy Chouinard to score. They had just acquired Steve Tambellini, and Jim Peplinski was coming off a thirty goal season. The question why did the Flames need Risebrough? was answered in short order when he made his debut in a Calgary uniform. Nobody's bothered to ask the question since. Risebrough became the Flames' most important centre, and some said, their most important player.

In short work, Fletcher traded Bridgman and Chouinard and released Tambellini. Nilsson was moved to the wing, then traded. Peplinski was moved to the wing permanently. If Lanny McDonald had given the Flames an identity when he first joined the club, Risebrough gave the club something else: an example. As time went on, their names would invariably be linked together. McDonald and Risebrough — the heart of the Flames.

Risebrough surprised almost everybody in his first year with the Flames by playing almost the entire regular season, the first time he had done so in five seasons. The next year he played in seventy-seven games and played a big part in the seven-game series the Flames lost to the Oilers. The trade to Calgary had given him new life, and he was taking advantage of it. The Flames showed promise in their 1984 playoff loss to the Oilers. Heading into the '84-85 season, Risebrough wanted to build on that. And summer was the time to do the building. When he was in just the right mood, Risebrough would get on his ten speed bicycle and pedal the undulating road from Calgary to Cochrane. He hadn't remembered ever feeling so healthy, so strong. He had never been overly muscled, but his body seemed better developed at age thirty than ever before. He would be ready for camp, ready to be in the kind of condition Bob Johnson wanted his players to report in. Never was Risebrough so ready. Never did a training camp end in such disappointment.

Early in camp, Risebrough was working out on one of the club's weight machines. He was doing leg exercises and was having no trouble with it. Suddenly, he pulled the weight with his thigh and his body shook. Something gave in his thigh. Doctors weren't sure what. All they knew was Risebrough couldn't skate. What began as a day to day injury became a week-to-week injury and eventually month-to-month. A season Risebrough had been so looking forward to had been ruined. "I'm past the point of going nuts," said Risebrough, who wasn't the only one frustrated by his inaction. Bob Johnson's problem as a coach was clear. He had no one to replace Risebrough.

Risebrough had become one of Johnson's most important players, for reasons that went beyond his on-ice presence. Whenever the Flames brought a rookie into the line-up, Johnson always had the same advice: watch Risebrough. When Kent Nilsson was in a slump, he would put Risebrough on his line. When Dan Quinn sulked, he would tell him to do what Risebrough did. In Johnson's mind, Risebrough was the consummate professional. The rest could learn from him. To Risebrough, every game was a big game. Every shift a big shift. He came out most nights and played his regular shift, took every important face-off, killed penalties, and played the occasional power-play shift. After the game, he would spend an hour untaping himself and icing the flesh beneath the tape.

The biggest problem of that wasted season was that the Flames didn't have him. And when he finally returned to the Flames' line-up, the season was almost over. The Flames were eliminated in the first round of the playoffs. The club was in need of changes, and Risebrough was already dealing with questions about retirement.

When the Flames opened their 1985-86 training camp in Moncton, Risebrough was one of the players being most closely watched. Unlike the last year, Risebrough had virtually taken the summer off. He didn't report to camp in his usual top-level condition. He hadn't really worked out. The thinking was, he could work himself into shape. Quietly, Flames' management indicated they didn't expect much from Risebrough. Thirty games would be a good season, someone said. Others wondered if he wasn't wasting his time. Playful jokes about retirement became part of the training camp language. "Shall we retire to the bus?" someone would ask Risebrough after a training camp workout. "Are you retiring so early?" he would be asked when heading to bed. Everyone was talking about the impending retirement of Risebrough. Except Risebrough. Whatever it was he didn't do in his summer of inactivity worked. Risebrough was ready to start and finish the season and he played most of the games in between.

In essence, the Flames brought him in without knowing the ultimate significance of the move. In some ways, that is primarily how the club was built. Partly by astute trading. Partly by astute drafting. Partly by luck. By the time Risebrough joined the Flames, some of the building groundwork had already been laid. Reggie Lemelin had signed as a free agent in 1978. Paul Reinhart, Jim Peplinski, and Tim Hunter were drafted in 1979. Hakan Loob, who didn't arrive until the start of the 1983 season, was drafted in 1980. The Flames traded

for McDonald in 1981 and drafted Al MacInnis and Mike
Vernon the same year. Risebrough was the first player traded
for in 1982.

Less than two months later, Fletcher made a curious deal.
The Flames had drafted winger Denis Cyr in the opening
round of the 1980 amateur draft. Two years later, their
patience had worn out. Cyr, a big scorer in junior hockey,
simply hadn't developed. He didn't do anything well enough
to warrant being in the NHL. The Flames knew it and they
knew he was still young enough to trade. The Chicago Black
Hawks were the only team really interested in Cyr, figuring
that if they could re-unite Cyr with his junior centreman,
Denis Savard, all would be well again. So Bob Pulford, the
Black Hawks' boss, went to work on Fletcher, trying to make a
deal for Cyr. In the end, Fletcher's asking price wasn't much.
The Flames only wanted the rights to a young Canadian centre
playing in Finland. At the time, they didn't know if the centreman would ever play for the Flames.

Carey Wilson wanted to be a doctor. Or he wanted to stay
in Europe. Or he wanted to play in the 1984 Olympic Games.
He wasn't sure what he wanted to do. He was in Finland,
playing for IFK Helsinki, when he first learned that his NHL
rights had been traded from the Black Hawks to the Flames.
He really didn't know what to think or what to say. Time, he
said, would answer all questions. In 1984, Wilson went on to
become one of the stars of Canada's Olympic hockey team
and following the Olympics, he joined the Flames. He's been a
regular ever since.

Not being blessed with early draft picks, the Flames had to
find another way to build. They went the pioneer route instead,
signing free agents, something that hardly followed conventional hockey thinking. The free agents signed in 1983
would later comprise a strong element of the club which

defeated Edmonton. Colin Patterson, who checked Jari Kurri into near submission in the Oiler series, was signed in 1983 out of Clarkson College. Neil Sheehy, the boxer from Harvard who was oddly but successfully matched against Gretzky, was signed the same year. So, too, were Jamie Macoun, who dropped out of Ohio State University to join the Flames, and Paul Baxter, who left the Pittsburgh Penguins on a technicality to become a free agent.

Patterson's signing was just another example of how fragile the entire hockey business is. He played in virtual obscurity at Clarkson, except that the Flames' scouts would drop by occasionally to watch the team play. The Flames wanted to monitor the development of a defenceman they'd chosen in the third round of the 1982 draft named Jim Laing. Laing played for Clarkson. Whenever a scout went to watch Laing, they came away talking about Patterson. Laing never made the Flames, but a little more than a year later, the Flames signed Patterson. Patterson came to training camp, but in Johnson's opinion, he wasn't ready to step into the line up. Instead, the Flames tried to lend him to the Canadian Olympic team. They weren't interested either. So Patterson was returned to the Flames and then cut for the third time in the pre-season. He wound up in the Central Hockey League. He played six games for Colorado and then was called up. Patterson's been there ever since.

In what could have been Jamie Macoun's draft year, the young defenceman divided his season between a couple of tier-two junior teams. In 1979, with a pro career the last thing on his mind, Macoun enrolled at Ohio State to play a little hockey and get an education. The fact that Macoun wasn't drafted meant he was a free agent and could sell his services to the highest bidder. If indeed there was a bidder. Two-and-a-half years after the fact, there was one: the Calgary Flames.

Without the free agents, the Flames would never have been so competitive so soon. Charles Bourgeois was signed in 1981, Eddy Beers was signed in 1982, and Gino Cavallini was signed in 1984. The three were later sent to St. Louis for Joey Mullen. But not everything worked out as planned along the way.

For every Patterson, Macoun, and Sheehy who has made it in the NHL, there were others who did not. The Flames, who had luck with the Swedish Nilsson and the Finnish defenceman Pekka Rautakallio, went back to Europe in search of further talent. They came back with two Finnish players, defenceman Kari Eloranta and forward Kari Jalonen. Both Eloranta and Jalonen had short and checkered professional careers. Eloranta was a Flame, then a St. Louis Blue, then a Flame again, before he eventually returned to Europe. Jalonen was a Flame for a brief time, and an Oiler for an even briefer stay. In time, Eloranta and Jalonen were forgotten, as were other free agent signings: Dan Kane, Bill Hobbins, Pierre Rioux, Mike Prestidge, and Gord Hampson.

The Flames were forced to become leaders in the free agent marketplace because they weren't especially successful at the drafting table. The 1979 draft, a shortened six-round excursion because of the merger with World Hockey Association teams, had turned out well for the Flames. With a late first-round pick, the Flames chose Paul Reinhart, who had played both centre and defence with the Kitchener Rangers. Reinhart, after debating about joining the Canadian Olympic team for the 1980 Games, instead joined the Flames in Atlanta. He had an impressive rookie season, and has been one of the best picks the club has made. Aside from back problems which have plagued his career in recent seasons, Reinhart has long been considered one of the league's best offensive defencemen. The Flames also thought they found a tough defenceman in that 1979 draft. They found tough. They didn't find defence. They found out later that Tim Hunter, chosen in the third round, was more suited to playing forward. His defence would come from the wing. The Flames fourth-round pick that year turned out to be a much more significant player.

When Jim Peplinski first came to the Flames' camp, he was a centre. He had played mostly right wing in junior, but the Flames had a shortage of centres that first season in Calgary. Peplinski played centre until Bob Johnson arrived as coach. Unimpressed with Peplinski's skating ability and his offensive skill, Johnson decided to move Peplinski back to his original position. Johnson liked Peplinski's size and his spirit, but he didn't know where to play him. Eventually, Johnson decided to make Peplinski one of his special projects and turned him into a competent left winger, a position more suited to his robust style and his ability to drive for the net.

If the 1979 draft turned out to be a good one, the 1980 draft turned out to be a disaster. The Flames salvaged some of the picks, first by dealing Cyr for Carey Wilson. Of their three second-round picks, only defenceman Steve Konroyd played up to expectations. Konroyd was utilized in the deal for John Tonelli. Of the other two, Tony Curtale was eventually released and Kevin LaVallee traded. The best of the bunch came out of the ninth round, when the Flames chose Hakan Loob. The drafting of Loob was another example of having to be good to be lucky. The Flames were smart enough to take him, but why did they wait so long to pick him? The LaVallee deal was another example of good timing, and turned out much better than anticipated. There didn't seem to be a coach anywhere who wasn't impressed with LaVallee's skill. He was quick, strong, had puck handling abilities, and could shoot. But somehow, he couldn't translate his skill from practice to the game. His greatest asset was his ability to frustrate coaches.

They didn't know what to do with him. LaVallee and Johnson
didn't get along and something had to be done. So the Flames
let it be known he was available and traded him to Los Angeles.
In return, they thought they were getting a goal scorer.

When Steve Bozek broke into the NHL in 1981 as the
left winger on a line with Marcel Dionne and Dave Taylor,
there was no stopping him. Charlie Simmer had been out with
a broken leg and the Los Angeles Kings needed someone to fill
in on the Triple Crown line. They turned to Bozek, a speedy
rookie from Northern Michigan. Bozek quickly took over
where Simmer had left off. He scored and scored and scored.
After an excellent rookie season, Fletcher, the Flames' general
manager, predicted Bozek would one day become a fifty goal
scorer in the league. Fletcher didn't know it would take more
than three seasons for Bozek to score his next fifty goals.

The LaVallee deal turned out to be a good one, not
because LaVallee bombed out in Los Angeles and later in St.
Louis, but because Bozek did not bomb out with the Flames.
He didn't become the scorer they thought he would be, but he
did become a viable, contributing member of the club. In
basketball, they'd call him the sixth man. In football, he'd be a
special team player. What Bozek became with the Flames was
their designated handyman. If they needed a centre, he played
centre. If they needed a winger, he played wing. If they needed
someone to sit out a game, Bozek sat out. He grew frustrated
in time, but he knew he had to keep his cool. Through the
Flames' successful playoff run, Bozek became an integral player.

The by-products of the 1980 draft turned out to be Loob,
Bozek, and Tonelli.

In the 1981 draft, the Flames were forced to learn that
patience could indeed be a virtue. Once again, the Flames'
hierarchy sat down on draft day with another pick in the
middle of the pack. They weren't picking high enough to get

the player they really wanted. Once again, they were drafting a project. The Flames knew who they figured to get, but weren't sure if they wanted Allan MacInnis. Before the draft, they said privately that if MacInnis, a defenceman from Kitchener, was available, they would take him. When the time came and MacInnis was available, the Flames hesitated. They called one time out, then another. They had trouble deciding between MacInnis and left winger Todd Strueby of Saskatoon. Finally they chose MacInnis. He is a regular, while Strueby has played only five NHL games to date.

However, it took MacInnis time to develop. He came to his first Flames' training camp and showed little. Like so many rookies, he left disappointed. He came back for his second camp and still didn't make the team. He was reaching that critical stage where he would soon become former prospect instead of future prospect. At his third camp, MacInnis again did not make the team. But nineteen games in the minor leagues were all the seasoning he needed. He joined the Flames for the final half of the 1983 - 84 season, and was a big part of the near-victory over the Oilers in the Smythe Division final. But for all he had accomplished offensively, especially with his slapshot — considered by some as the hardest in hockey — there were still questions about MacInnis. He had knee problems, which worried the Flames' coaches and management. He was good with the puck, not so good without it. He was strong offensively, but still learning on defence. He was big, but not physical. Strong on his skates, but not quick. For every positive, MacInnis offered a negative. In time, some of his shortcomings became apparent. There had been rumours the Flames had tried to trade MacInnis, but nothing happened. Then, almost suddenly, in this third NHL season, some of his problems started to disappear. The one-dimensional defenceman became two-dimensional. No longer was there talk of trading MacInnis. He was part of the future.

MacInnis was not the only plum to come out of the 1981 draft. The Flames made a popular move by selecting Mike Vernon from the Calgary Wranglers in the third round. Vernon had twice been most valuable player in the Western Hockey League and the local fans knew him and liked him. Like MacInnis, he would take time to make it to the NHL. Unlike MacInnis, he became a Flame because of a deal which was made before the Flames had ever moved to Calgary. In their final season in Atlanta, with the franchise in deep trouble, the Flames went out and signed Jim Craig, the gold medal winning goaltender from the 1980 U.S. Olympic team, to a pro contract. They needed Craig's name to sell tickets and he packed them into The Omni twice for games he started. Craig won his debut against the Winnipeg Jets, then the worst team in the league. In his second start, he gave up five goals to the New York Islanders and was pulled out of the game. The Flames gave him the rest of the season off, explaining he was "exhausted" from the rigours of the Olympic year. It proved to be an effective smokescreen. When the Flames moved north, they didn't need Craig anymore. Instead, they traded him to the goalie-poor Boston Bruins for two draft picks. One was used on Steve Konroyd. The other was used to select Vernon. In exchange for Craig, a player they didn't want, they eventually wound up with John Tonelli and Vernon, the most successful playoff goaltender the club has ever had.

One of the shortcomings of the entry draft is it leaves clubs open to second guessing. What would have happened if the Flames had selected Todd Streuby instead of Al MacInnis? Or Brent Sutter instead of Denis Cyr? Normally, each pick comes down to a choice between two players. There is rarely a consensus among club scouts as to which player to pick. When the Flames were trying to compile their draft list prior to the

1983 draft, they were having difficulties. Because the Flames were using Buffalo's first-rounder, they were choosing in the second half of the draft again. They didn't expect to get a player who could step right into the line-up. They also knew they'd likely wind up with a centre. The scouts, fresh from watching the national junior hockey championships, the Memorial Cup, were impressed with an American centreman named Alfie Turcotte. The thinking was that Turcotte would likely be available by the time the Flames were picking. Heading into the draft, the Flames figured Turcotte would be their man. Cliff Fletcher didn't agree. After years of disappointing drafts, Fletcher brought in a new staff, headed by Gerry Blair. Jack Ferreira would handle his U.S. scouting. Both have proved to be valuable additions. Fletcher also decided he would take a more active role in choosing players. If someone was going to be wrong, it was going to be him. On draft day, they still weren't sure who to take. Turcotte was available. Some of the Flames' staff wanted him. Fletcher didn't. Putting himself publicly on the line, Fletcher decided to pick Dan Quinn from the Belleville Bulls. Turcotte was drafted by Montreal. Years later, he was traded to Edmonton. Quinn didn't make the Flames in his first training camp but he made a big impression. Halfway through the season, he joined the team and he's been at centre ever since. That same year, the Flames also came up with centreman Perry Berezan in the third round. Berezan was chosen with a selection acquired from Washington Capitals in the deal for goalie Pat Riggin.

What began in 1978 with the signing of Reggie Lemelin culminated in 1986 with the trade for John Tonelli. While there were no five-year plans, no overall design — the building of the Flames was a culmination of many moves. The naming of Bob Johnson as coach in 1982. The trades for McDonald, Risebrough, and Mullen. The free agents who worked out and those who did not. In the end, the Flames put it all together to compile one of hockey's deepest rosters, a roster deep enough and strong enough to send hockey's most talented team, the Edmonton Oilers, to the golf course on May 1.

7
The Goalies

"If three factors are important, the first is goaltending, the second is goaltending and the third is special teams."
PAUL REINHART'S PLAYOFF CHECKLIST

In the days leading up to the playoffs, the most intriguing question centred on the Flames' goaltending. Coach Bob Johnson had a decision to make and he wasn't in a decisive mood. Would he start the proven commodity, Reggie Lemelin, a thirty game winner the year before and the clear No. 1 when the season began? Or would he gamble on the unknown, rookie Mike Vernon, a player with not a single minute of play-off experience, the man who began the year as the fourth goaltender on the depth chart?

Complicating matters was the fact that both players were headed in different directions. Lemelin, the logical choice, starred in the early season, slumped in the middle, and was missing a crispness to his play as the season wound down. Vernon, on the other hand, had been slowly coming along, moving up to Calgary from Moncton when injuries and an unnatural tendency to dehydration forced Marc D'Amour out of the line-up. As the Flames prepared for a first-round meeting with the Winnipeg Jets, a team that Lemelin had dominated throughout his career, Johnson couldn't decide.

Much depended on his decision. One year earlier, when the same two teams met, Lemelin made a costly error in the first game, one that allowed the Jets to win a game they were ready to lose, one that gave the Jets an important leg up in the short series. Moreover, the Flames couldn't afford another quick playoff exit. Even though they had established a pack of team records the year before — including most wins, most road wins, and most points — their summary dismissal in the first round was all that people remembered. The Jets were barely a reasonable facsimile of the team that played so well the year before and that scared the Flames. Winnipeg could do a lot towards salvaging a dismal season by knocking off Calgary.

The last week of the season made up Johnson's mind for him. Johnson, figuring to go with Lemelin all the way, changed his mind when the thirty-one-year-old struggled in a 6-5 win over the Vancouver Canucks. Johnson decided to throw Vernon to the wolves two nights later when the Flames played the Oilers, looking for their first win of the season over Edmonton. Surprise, surprise, surprise. The Flames defeated the Oilers with ease and Vernon, though not the main reason they won, acquitted himself well. Even Lemelin read the writing on the wall. "I can see what's happening," he said. "I've been around." Vernon would be the starter until he faltered. For Reggie Lemelin, it would be a long wait.

Reggie Lemelin didn't play much in training camp. He didn't need to. After years of looking over his shoulder, checking out the competition, the Flames had decided to leave Lemelin alone this season. They were convinced — finally — that Lemelin could be the team's full-time goaltender. They took a lot of convincing. Never mind that five years earlier, in his first year in Calgary, Lemelin did not lose a single game on home ice. Or that two years earlier, he finished second to Tom Barrasso in the Vezina Trophy balloting. Or that last year, he finished third in the voting, posted a 30-12-10 record, a 3.46 goals-against average and a .889 save percentage. It wasn't until Don Edwards, a player who'd gone four months the previous year without winning a game, forced a showdown with general manager Cliff Fletcher and asked for more guaranteed playing time that the Flames decided to go with Lemelin as their No. 1 goaltender. Lemelin would play 75 per cent of the games and help tutor whichever one of the three untried rookies that had won a spot on the major-league roster.

The Flames' decision to dump Edwards made Lemelin's summer. Until Lemelin put together back-to-back brilliant seasons, Fletcher never really thought that the veteran goaltender could handle the top job. Fletcher used to talk about what a solid back-up Lemelin could be. He gave up a king's ransom in draft choices and in draft priorities to get Edwards from the Buffalo Sabres. With so much invested in Edwards and so little in Lemelin, it took the Flames three full seasons to decide that they were better off with what they had — Reggie Lemelin — than with someone else's cast-off. Edwards received more second chances than Muhammad Ali. No matter how hard he worked, no matter how many times the Flames tried to railroad Edwards into the line-up, he failed in meeting the goaltender's prime directive: he didn't stop enough pucks.

By contrast, Lemelin had become one of the most popular athletes ever to play in Calgary. His easy-going nature, his history of drawing the short straw, made him popular in an Everyman sort of way. He spent much of his career in the wrong place at the wrong time. That made him an easy player to cheer for, a Horatio Alger on skates that finally hit the big time in a big way and was determined to stay there.

All along, Lemelin's major problem was proving to people he belonged. In Calgary, the second part of his story was common knowledge — how the Flames put him on waivers in 1982, how any team in the league could have claimed him for $10,000, how none did, how Lemelin, finally given the opportunity to play, won his first game and then kept on winning. The politics in his life started much sooner. In 1978, Lemelin was faced with a career crisis. The past summer, Philadelphia Flyers, a team knee-deep in goaltending prospects, gave him his outright release.

No NHL team expressed an interest, so Lemelin signed a minor-league contract with the Philadelphia Firebirds of the North American Hockey League. Then, just before the season was to begin, the NAHL folded. So the Firebirds, a collection of non-prospects and end-of-the-line players, were absorbed by the American Hockey League, a definite cut above the level they were to play. Lemelin started the Firebirds' opener against Maine, the Flyers' No. 1 minor-league affiliate, and played sensationally in a 5-1 win. Lemelin can recite his statistics from that season on a moment's notice: 31 wins, 21 losses, 9 ties, a 2.95 goals-against average, 4 shutouts, first all-star team and half-a-dozen inquiries from NHL teams.

Lemelin chose the Atlanta Flames because it looked as if they had an opening. The Flames traded Phil Myre the previous year and had only Yves Belanger, Lemelin's junior teammate, as a back-up to Dan Bouchard. Lemelin won the job ahead of Belanger in 1978-79 and looked set to go. Then disaster struck again. The World Hockey Association was in its death throes and after years of bitter negotiations, four teams were absorbed into the NHL. To gain admission, WHA teams were allowed to protect only two players from their rosters. The rest reverted to the NHL teams holding their rights. So Pat Riggin of the Birmingham Bulls and the Flames' second-round choice in 1979, joined Atlanta in 1979. Riggin was in. Lemelin was out.

Then, early in 1980, came the Winter Olympics in Lake Placid. Around February, the Flames — by now, dying at the gate — found themselves in possession of a genuine, wrapped-in-the-flag hero in Jim Craig, goaltender of the U.S. Olympic team. The Flames need a box-office fix and Craig provided it. Riggin was demoted to the press box as the No. 3 goaltender and Lemelin dropped another place in the pecking order. Ultimately, Lemelin's big break came the year Georgia businessman Tom Cousins sold the Flames to Vancouver entrepreneur Nelson Skalbania who moved the team to Calgary. Craig became dispensible and was dispensed to the Boston Bruins for a pair of draft choices. Bouchard hated Calgary. Five weeks into the season, he quit the team and demanded a trade. Lemelin came up as his replacement and has been with the team ever since.

Lemelin played for a year and a half with the Flames until the next crisis came. That was in 1982 when Al MacNeil was replaced by Bob Johnson as coach and Fletcher acquired Edwards from the Sabres, dumping Riggin one day later. Johnson liked the work in training camp of minor-leaguer Tim Bernhardt and once again, Lemelin found himself No. 3 and trying harder.

"It was like a nightmare coming back to haunt you," said Lemelin. "When Riggin came in, I lost my job. Now they bring Edwards in and I lose my job again. It was exactly the same situation, a new goalie and a new coach each time. Johnson was from U.S. college. I'm sure the first thing he said was: 'Who's Lemelin? Never heard of him.' He's coaching in college. He probably didn't have a clue who I was. He would have just known the big names. So I found myself sitting in the stands. The only thing that saved me was my contract.

But once I started to play, he learned who I was because he watched me play. That was the frustrating part, having to show yourself constantly again and again to a different guy.''

What bothered Lemelin was that no one took his successes seriously, but hammered away whenever he faltered. ''A lot of people who have watched hockey for a long time still don't believe I'm for real. To them, I'm still the old back-up. They think: 'Ah, he's not so good.' What are you going to do? There are times when it's disappointing because you think you've done enough to be recognized, but what can you do? You can't fight the system. People always go back to the old story. That's what they want to hear.''

By the start of the 1985-86 season, the Flames sounded convinced. Fletcher received a chance to invest in some goal-tending insurance when the agent for veteran netminder Giles Meloche called and asked if the Flames were interested. Fletcher said no. If they had wanted Meloche, they could have kept Edwards. Lemelin was turning thirty-one and the Flames thought it was the logical time to bring in a young goaltender. It was risky, but then risk was a part of professional sport. Adding Meloche would not help the team in the long run. If the worst possible scenario unfolded — Lemelin suffering an injury, the young goaltenders proving unable to handle the job — the Flames could always pick up an experienced net-minder once the season began.

In the battle for the back-up spot, there were three candidates: Rick Kosti, Marc D'Amour, and Mike Vernon. The Flames convinced Kosti, a free agent, to drop out of the University of Minnesota-Duluth to compete for the opening in goal. It looked like a once-in-a-lifetime chance for him. The day after the Flames signed Kosti, they traded Edwards. Somebody was going to get that second job and the Flames convinced Kosti he had as good a chance as anyone else. D'Amour, who signed as a free agent in 1983, was the No. 1 goaltender for the Flames' No. 1 minor-league club, the Moncton Golden Flames. Prior to Moncton, D'Amour did time in the International League and for much of the 1983-84 season, looked like a non-prospect. But his year in Moncton made him a legitimate contender for the open spot. Then there was Vernon. The only one of the three goaltenders drafted by the Flames, Vernon was a two-time Western Hockey League most-valuable player. He was thought to be their goaltender of the future — until he stumbled in Moncton. Suddenly, he couldn't stop the puck. He was twenty-two, a home-town boy with impressive credentials. Now that his chance was finally upon him, he was in a tight, three-way fight for the place on the roster. Nothing that happened in his most recent season suggested he was the man for the job.

Ten days into training camp, Johnson was disappointed. In games, in scrimmages, in a hastily scheduled intra-squad game, not one of the three candidates made much of an impression.

''All they're doing is making my job more difficult,'' said Johnson. ''No one is really winning the job, are they?'' In Johnson's rating system (one means excellent, five means poor), Vernon graded out as a four in his first pre-season start. D'Amour, who came on in relief, received a three. Kosti, whose pre-season debut against the Nordiques in Quebec was a disaster, received a chance to make some badly needed points with Johnson during the team's intra-squad game. Instead, he gave up six goals in sixty minutes and had Johnson asking: ''Was he playing? I didn't know he was playing. Nothing caught my eye. I watched very carefully. On a Sunday morning, in that kind of game, things have got to happen. They have to catch your eye. I can't do it for them. They've got to do it for themselves.''

Earlier, Kosti allowed a weak, fluttering shot from far out to elude him for the winning goal in his NHL pre-season debut. He wasn't sharp any time during camp, but his nervousness was the most disconcerting development. Even when he stopped the puck, he didn't look too sure of himself. When the Flames broke camp in Moncton, they left Kosti behind. They wanted him to be the starting goaltender on their top farm team so he could gain maximum experience in a minimum amount of time. D'Amour and Vernon were left to play for No. 2 and No. 4.

Both of them improved as camp progressed, but neither pulled ahead. The difference in their respective save percentages was a scant five one-thousandths of a point and that, as much as anything, illustrated how close the race was. The day before the season began, Johnson made a difficult but reasonable decision. He chose D'Amour. As a coach, Johnson's history was to reward players for performance. D'Amour's performance the past year in the minor-leagues was the only way he could legitimately separate the two.

"It was one of those decisions where you could flip a coin and not have a loser," explained Johnson. "This is not necessarily a lasting decision. We just threw the ball to him first." For D'Amour, the verdict was bittersweet. Against long odds, he had won the job — but he won it at the expense of a close friend. He wanted to celebrate, but without Vernon, it didn't seem right. "I feel bad for Mike," said D'Amour. "I wish him luck. He's a super goalie."

Because the Flames were sharing their minor-league affiliate with the Boston Bruins that season, they could only place one goaltender in Moncton. That forced them to send Vernon to Salt Lake City of the International Hockey league — one step below the calibre of play in the American League. The thinking was that Vernon fell into a rut in Moncton. Perhaps a

change of scenery and a chance to work with a new coach —
Wayne Thomas, a former NHL goaltender — would get
Vernon's career back on track. Plus, it meant a raise. Vernon
would get his salary in U.S. dollars, not Canadian. Vernon
tried to look on the bright side. He wouldn't have got much
work in Calgary anyway. Not with Lemelin established as the
No. 1 goaltender. In the IHL, he would play a lot.

As advertised, Lemelin played almost all the games in the
first two months. D'Amour made his regular-season debut
against Edmonton on the 25th of October and showed Johnson
enough to get a second start against the Buffalo Sabres five
nights later. If the Oilers represented a monkey on the Flames'
back, then the Sabres were an albatross around their necks.
Calgary hadn't beaten Buffalo since they had moved to the
Olympic Saddledome from the Stampede Corral. D'Amour —
nicknamed Shakey by his teammates in junior hockey — was
everything but, stopping thirty-four shots as the Flames
recorded a 4-2 win. Clearly, Johnson wasn't picking his spots.
D'Amour wasn't exactly being eased into the league with a
bunch of games against the NHL's softies. ''It's eighty
games,'' said Johnson. ''I have to find out if he can play.''

D'Amour, a pleasing, out-going character on the outside,
was strung as tight as piano wire on the inside. He suffered
from the Glenn Hall disease: acute nervousness before and
during every game. Hence the nickname Shakey. He'd get the
jitters so bad, it became a tangible, physical thing. ''I'm getting
better,'' he said, following the win over Buffalo. ''Before, I
was just awful. I couldn't drink a full glass of pop in the
dressing room because it would spill over. I'd have to fill it
half full.''

With D'Amour providing competent work as the No. 2
man and Lemelin finding his form in November, the Flames
were getting what they wanted out of their goaltenders.

Lemelin scored his biggest personal win of the season when he defeated the Nordiques in Quebec 3-1, the first time in his life that he had won a game in his hometown. It was a special night for him because, as a goalie, Quebec City had never been his kind of town. The system was working. Then the Flames hit the skids in mid-December and the goaltending, like everything else, came apart. Throughout his career, Lemelin prided himself on the number of wins he posted in a year. Goaltenders, like starting pitchers in baseball, could be roughed up early, but get in the groove and they'd make the key save with the game on the line. Suddenly, Lemelin couldn't win the games he used to win going away, and it was bothering him.

Later, after the slump had gone into the record books, Lemelin would comment: "I didn't have a good game against Vancouver when it started. It seemed everything got worse after that and everybody looked for a scapegoat, someone to blame it on. All of a sudden, I find out it's my fault. It seems that since that time, people are really asking questions about me. I started every game but one during the whole streak. By then, I think it would have been time to give the other goaltenders a chance because the pressure was pretty heavy on everybody, especially the guy at the end. But I hung in there and played my games and it seemed to get worse and worse. Since then, we're definitely back in the right order, but there are still a lot of skeptical thoughts in the air you can feel all the time."

When the team finally did get in the win column, Vernon — called up the day before — picked up the victory. The Flames, for the first time in years, went on the road with three goaltenders in tow. Johnson said Lemelin would be on a week's vacation. Vernon and D'Amour would do the bulk of the work. Vernon started the first of five road games with a respectable showing in a 3-0 loss to Philadelphia. D'Amour received the call three nights later in Washington. Halfway through the game, he began to cramp up, ostensibly because he was dehydrating in the heat of the Capital Centre. Lemelin replaced him, played well, and won the game. Abruptly, his vacation ended. Vernon went back to the minors. D'Amour stayed up in essentially the same capacity as before.

One week later, D'Amour's season would come to an end in a wholly capricious way. New Jersey Devils paid a visit to the Saddledome and D'Amour received the start because Lemelin was down with the flu. Halfway through the game, the Flames — ahead 6-2 — were cruising to an easy win. Then it happened. Just as he did against the Capitals, D'Amour began to cramp up. Lemelin was so sick he couldn't even sit on the bench. Had D'Amour been unable to finish, the Flames had a junior goaltender waiting in the wings inside their dressing room. Johnson didn't need to go to him. D'Amour, looking like a boxer on the ropes waiting for the final bell to sound, gave up four third-period goals as the Devils earned a 6-6 tie. D'Amour was packed off to hospital after the game so doctors could conduct tests on him. No one knew exactly what was wrong, but Johnson was getting worried.

''We're very concerned,'' he said. ''We've got to make a decision. This is ridiculous. We can't afford to have this happen. I wanted to get the one guy in there (Lemelin) and he says he can't go. The other guy (D'Amour), he's dying on us out there but I had to keep him in. They could easily have gotten another one. If they had put it on net, they would have gotten another one. They missed the net on the last couple.''

''I don't know what it is,'' said D'Amour. ''Something's wrong. It happened before, but not two games in a row like this. It happened in junior, it happened in the CHL, it happened in the AHL. Now, you come into these buildings, there's more people, it's hotter, I don't know, something's got to be done.''

D'Amour stayed in hospital until 3:30 the next morning undergoing tests. In the meantime, doctors had him on intravenous so they could pump back into him some of the fluids he lost the night before. He dropped eleven pounds in one game. As the Flames petitioned the league to allow them to tie water bottles to the top of the goal — so D'Amour could get a drink at any stoppage in play — the test results came back: apparently, D'Amour's frequent trips to the bench for water was causing the cramping.

"It is a worry," said D'Amour. "It's tough on me and tough on the guys. They see it happening and they start to second-guess me. That's the most important thing now, getting their confidence back in me. Hopefully, I'll get the matter straightened out in the next few days. Basically, what they want to do is piece together what's wrong and then do what they can for me."

Compounding D'Amour's troubles was the fact that he suffered a groin injury in practice a few days later. Vernon came up for the third time in five weeks and this time, he would not be dislodged from the roster. Slowly, he played himself into the picture. He picked up his first NHL shutout on February 21 against the Vancouver Canucks, stopping twenty-four shots. Two days later, he took the loss in a 6-2 decision to the Chicago Black Hawks, but it would be the last game he would lose as a starting goaltender until the second round of the playoffs. Meanwhile, D'Amour recovered. Though he played one more game against Detroit — a 3-3 tie, the last game before the trading deadline — he spent the remainder of the regular season in Moncton.

Without question, Vernon's breakthrough came on the second to last night of the season. That night, the Flames defeated Edmonton for the first time all year. He stopped twenty-six shots in a 9-3 win and earned third star. The win raised his record in recent starts to 6-0-1. More importantly, it gave the Oilers and coach Johnson something to think about. The first time Vernon ever played against Edmonton, he gave up four goals on six shots in eleven minutes and the experience will live with him forever. Under ''record, 1983-84 season'' is Vernon's goals-against average for the season — 21.82. He needed to prove something to himself and he did.

Lemelin actually finished the season with twenty-nine wins, good for a third-place tie with Buffalo's Tom Barrasso. However, in the final four weeks, Lemelin registered only a 1-5 record. Vernon, by contrast, ended with a six-week undefeated streak and a 3-0 record against Winnipeg, the Flames' first-round opponent.

Ultimately, Vernon's play would prove once again that the days of good goaltenders and bad goaltenders are a thing of the past. Now, there are only hot goaltenders and cold goaltenders.

''Goaltending is a funny thing,'' said Vernon. ''It's not really the same as the forwards or defencemen. Goaltending is based on confidence and concentration. Once you have that, you don't get uptight. Even if you do give up a bad goal, you put it behind you. You say: 'On to the next one.' Confidence may be an overused word, but it's the key word for a goaltender.''

8
The Rookies

"Usually with a young defenceman, it takes two or three years before he even has a clue.... I've seen Gary Suter make some plays that you just don't expect to see from a rookie defenceman." **PAUL BAXTER**

The tug-of-war over Gary Suter started early. On the second day of training camp, third-year defenceman Al MacInnis — watching from the stands, looking over the competition in the Moncton Coliseum — nodded towards a five-foot-eleven defenceman and mentally gave him the job. Calgary Flames started with an opening on defence, the result of Kari Eloranta's decision to play in Europe. Up to four rookies were given a chance to fill the opening, but forty-eight hours into the competition, MacInnis figured the race was over. The job belonged to Suter. Turns out, MacInnis was psychic. Or possibly he just saw what everyone else in the organization eventually came to see as well: that this longshot, this afterthought, this ninth-round draft choice who nobody wanted in 1982, would become a player that any team could have used in 1986. Suter was a blond, stocky defenceman, a little on the short side, but with more on-ice presence than anyone since Paul Reinhart's debut in 1979.

In the beginning, Suter was a quiet, almost withdrawn

person off the ice, but on the ice, he had impact right away. When Suter scored twice in the Flames' 9-2 win over the Los Angeles Kings in the second game of the season, coach Bob Johnson let it slip. Suter's start in hockey came courtesy of Johnson. From age ten to age twelve, Suter attended the Colorado hockey schools Johnson runs every year. Johnson figured that's where Suter learned to shoot the puck. Some time later, when it became clear that Suter was going to be another one of the Flames' shot-in-the-dark player finds, Ian McKenzie, the team's co-ordinator of scouting, explained how the team stumbled across Suter.

Suter became eligible for the NHL's entry draft in 1982, the year he turned eighteen. Two hundred and fifty-two players were chosen in the draft that year, but Suter wasn't one of them. He was eligible again the next year, 1983. Once again, 252 players were chosen. Suter wasn't one of them. McKenzie thought teams shied away from Suter because the league's Central Scouting service listed him as a relatively short, five-foot-nine defenceman. Nobody needed a five-foot-nine defenceman in today's NHL, no matter how talented he may be. Suter was five-nine — in 1982. By 1984, he was five-eleven and filling out as a sophomore player at the University of Wisconsin.

The story McKenzie likes to tell is about the day he was waiting outside the Wisconsin dressing room following a game. "I was standing there when this kid walked by," said McKenzie. "I said: Who's that? Somebody answered: Suter, that's Suter. I couldn't believe it. He wasn't five-nine. He was as tall as I was. I told Cliff we better send somebody down there to watch him because he's bigger than we think."

In the end, the Flames' good luck — they finally selected him in the ninth round of the 1984 entry draft — cost Suter money. Had he been passed over for one more year, he would have become a free agent. Conceivably, he could have knocked down a $1 million contract. All twenty-one NHL teams missed Suter the first time because he played high school hockey for the Culver Military Academy in Plymouth, Indiana as an eighteen-year-old. As a nineteen-year-old, Suter moved to the Dubuque Fighting Saints of the Midwestern Junior League. Neither team is a priority stop on the circuit that hockey scouts usually travel.

Not until Suter accepted a scholarship at the University of Wisconsin did he begin to attract some attention. In coach Johnson, the Flames had a connection with Wisconsin. Prior to joining Calgary in the summer of 1981, Johnson spent fifteen years coaching the Badgers. Two of Suter's older brothers, Bob and John, played for Johnson at Wisconsin. Johnson knew the family well, but hadn't seen Gary play for half-a-dozen years.

When the Flames approached Suter with a contract towards the end of the 1985 season, it turned out to be an unpopular move in Madison, Wisconsin, where the university is based. Johnson was considered something of a folk hero there because he turned a mediocre hockey program into a national power. Johnson's teams won three national championships. His successor, Jeff Sauer, was slowly rebuilding. With Suter, he thought he had a chance to add a national title to Johnson's three in the upcoming season. Without Suter, the chances were substantially reduced. So Johnson was in a bind. His head told him Suter was ready. His heart told him to leave him in Madison. His head won out.

With Johnson staying deep in the background, the Flames convinced Suter to leave school and turn pro. Suter made the decision to sign following an impressive performance in the 1985 world hockey championships. Playing for Team U.S.A., Suter was able to measure his skills against some of the world's finest players, from North American professionals to the top international players from Czechoslovakia and the Soviet Union. Team Canada included Steve Konroyd and Jamie Macoun, two players Suter would be competing against on the left side of the Flames' defence. Team U.S.A. included two players, Mike O'Connell of the Boston Bruins and Moe Mantha of the Pittsburgh Penguins, who were considered above average pro defencemen. When Suter was selected as one of Team U.S.A.'s three most valuable players, he knew the time had come to move on. By the time the Flames training camp ended, Suter had stepped into the line-up and impressed everyone with his poise. He just didn't play like a rookie. Johnson discovered he had an uncoachable sixth sense about the game and put him on the power play. Suter became a fixture there. Ten games into the season, Johnson handed out the first of eight report cards the players would receive over the course of the year. Suter emerged as the top defenceman on the team. Even his peers realized it.

Said defenceman Paul Baxter: ''He's been our best defenceman by a mile. I'm sure the expectations for him were high, but they were nowhere near what he's accomplished so far. He's making plays out there that Paul Coffey or Doug Wilson would be proud of. Especially on the power-play.''

''He is consistent,'' added Pierre Page, the assistant coach. ''That's usually a rare quality in so young a player. The main value of a player is his consistency — game in, game out; home and on the road; the way he plays in clutch games. Right now, so far, he's been a pleasant surprise.''

Suter didn't stop surprising the coaching staff. Midway through the season, in response to the team's eleven game slump, the Flames borrowed a page from the Edmonton Oilers' playbook and began revamping their offence. Instead of playing so conservatively, they asked their defencemen to join the offence. They were looking for an edge. From watching tapes of the Oilers, they decided to use Suter the way the Oilers used Paul Coffey: as an offensive threat. They decided to take more chances and move a defenceman into the attack, trying to turn three-on-three rushes into four-on-threes.

Under the new system, Suter blossomed. In the first half, he scored a respectable twenty-three points. In the second half, he scored forty-five. Only one defenceman in league history, Larry Murphy, accumulated more scoring points than the sixty-eight Suter put on the board in the regular season — more than Bobby Orr, more than Denis Potvin, more than Paul Coffey. In the end, the better Suter became, the more the Flames thought they could give up Konroyd — once considered an untouchable commodity, a defensive defenceman — to add a new dimension to the team for their playoff run. The new dimension was called John Tonelli.

By March, the Flames had only one real complaint about the way Suter's rookie season was going: the fact that he was doing it in such relative anonymity. Johnson may have inadvertently contributed to that in February when he questioned Glen Sather's decision to add Suter to the NHL all-star team — ahead of Reggie Lemelin and Lanny McDonald, Johnson's choices. The Flames thought Sather's decision to choose Suter was a subtle put-down of their club — that the only Calgary player good enough to play in the All-Star Game was a twenty-one-year-old rookie.

Moreover, in Toronto, the lobbying for Wendel Clark's rookie-of-the-year bid had become louder. The Maple Leafs, a team that previously didn't know the meaning of the term public relations, sensed they had a winner in Clark, the pugnacious left winger with the heavy wrist shot.

In March, they started an impressive campaign to support Clark's Calder Trophy candidacy. They bombarded voting

The faceshields square off, Joe Mullen and Guy Carbonneau (21).

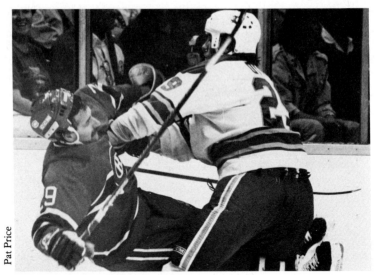

Joel Otto (29) gets the best of Gaston Gingras.

Doug Risebrough at his antagonizing best.

Gary Suter showing some of his Calder Trophy winning form.

John Tonelli (27) congratulated by Paul Reinhart, after scoring in
Game 1 of the Stanley Cup finals.

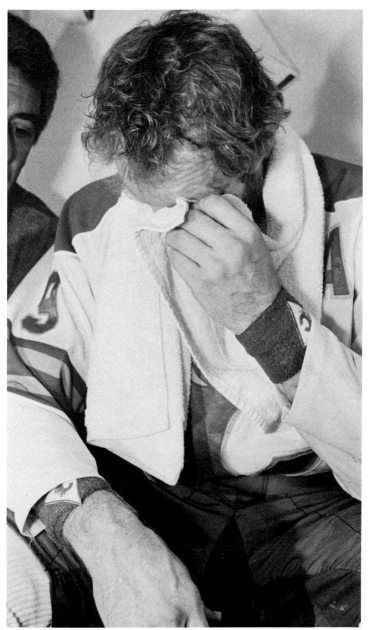

On the night the season ended, Lanny McDonald didn't look up.

Jubilation: the Badger and Lanny rejoice as the Flames eliminated the St. Louis Blues.

Badger Bob, at home, at practice.

Lanny celebrates his 1984 overtime goal which sends the Edmonton series to a seventh game.

Neil Sheehy (5) studied ballet before the last NHL season.

Pat Price

The legend and his student: Glenn Hall (r) and Reggie Lemelin.

Pat Price

The Great One, Wayne Gretzky, doesn't look so great here.

Pat Price

Jamie Macoun had the best chance to send Game 5 of the finals into overtime with less than a minute remaining.

Doug Risebrough (1) and Jim Peplinski hold up Clarence Campbell Cup.

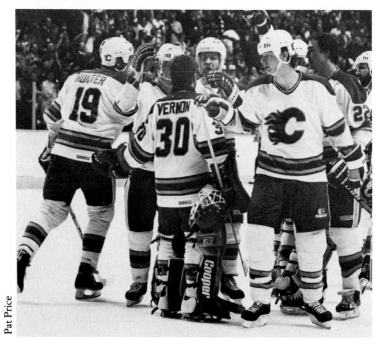

Flames win Game 1 of the finals.

Guy Carbonneau crosses the goal line, but the puck doesn't.

Thousands mob Stampede Grounds for final Flames' rally.

Mike Eaves, showing off his goaltending abilities, during a Stanley Cup practice session.

Mike Vernon started on his comeback trail with a victory over the Moscow Dynamo.

Pat Price

Mike Vernon and Dan Quinn after Game 1 Stanley Cup final win.

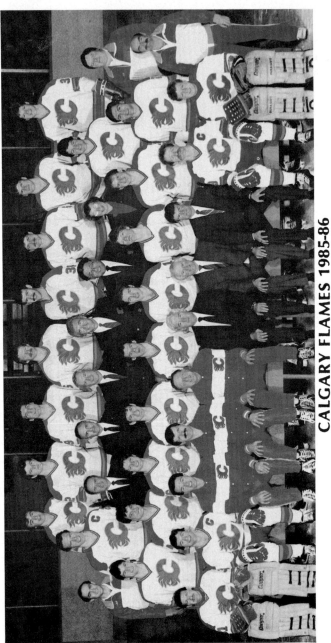

CALGARY FLAMES 1985-86

First Row: (left to right) Rejean Lemelin, Doug Risebrough, co-captain; Pierre Page, asst. coach; Bob Murdoch, asst. coach; Bob Johnson, head coach; Cliff Fletcher, president & general manager; Al MacNeil, asst. general manager, Al Coates, asst. to president & dir. marketing; Lanny McDonald, co-captain; Mike Vernon. **Second Row:** Perry Berezan, Paul Baxter, Steve Bozek, Hakan Loob, Joe Mullen, Dan Quinn, Gary Suter, Colin Patterson, John Tonelli, Jim Murray, trainer. **Third Row:** Al Murray, asst. trainer; Jim Peplinski, co-captain; Byron Seaman, Daryl Seaman, Harley Hotchkiss, Norman Green, Norman Kwong, Sonia Scurfield, owners; Paul Reinhart, Bobby Stewart, equipment manager. **Fourth Row:** Nick Fotiu, Allan MacInnis, Tim Hunter, Terry Johnson, Jamie Macoun, Neil Sheehy, Joel Otto, Carey Wilson.

members of the Professional Hockey Writer's Association with press releases praising Clark. It looked to be working. Clark was an impressive physical player, a moustachioed teenager that reminded people in Toronto of another prairie teenager that the Leafs let slip through their fingers: Lanny McDonald. Until playoff time, Clark was the only good news to emerge from that beleaguered organization all year. Meantime, Suter started with four strikes against him: he was a defenceman, he was a low draft choice, he wasn't especially chatty, and he played in Calgary. Only three defencemen in the last twenty-two years of the award had even won the Calder Trophy: Bobby Orr, Denis Potvin, and Ray Bourque. Unlike Clark, Suter was not a No. 1 draft choice. Suter preferred to let his play do the talking, especially early in the season, and that kept him from getting much exposure. Plus, Suter played in Calgary, a team that had one of the lowest profiles and represented one of the poorest road draws in the league. "It started with Reggie and right down the line, our players have been shortchanged," complained coach Bob Johnson. "It's partly the geography. Because of the time difference, they don't even know the score of our games in the East before they go to bed."

Suter made perhaps his biggest move of the year in the second last game of the season, a 9-3 win over Edmonton. That night, he scored six points. The six points moved him past three players — Bourque, Chris Chelios, Phil Housley — on the all-time scoring list for rookie defencemen. In the minds of many voters, Suter's eleventh-hour charge changed everything. The twenty-one-year-old from Madison was having a career year for rookie defencemen. Clark could arguably be considered a better prospect, possibly even a better long-range pro, but the definition of the award was fairly specific. The Calder Trophy went "to the player selected as most proficient in his first year of competition in the National Hockey League."

In an era when recent Calder Trophy winners such as Peter Stastny, Dale Hawerchuk, and Mario Lemieux posted 100-point rookie seasons as a matter of course, Clark — with thirty-four goals and only twelve assists — simply didn't possess numbers that were comparable to Suter's.

In the end, the only surprise in the voting was Suter's overwhelming margin of victory. He picked up thirty-five of sixty first-place votes and won going away. The Calder Trophy provided Suter with a hard-earned consolation prize. On the day the Flames eliminated the Oilers, Suter was forced to swallow a bitter pill. Although he made a major contribution to the upset win, he would be forced to watch the rest of the action from the sidelines. Oilers' centre Mark Messier ran Suter into the boards in the first period of the seventh game. Suter sat on the bench for the second, but a between-periods examination showed he wouldn't return — not for the third period, not for the St. Louis series, not until the Flames opened training camp for the 1986-87 season. "What a way to end the season," said Suter, fighting the twin emotions of elation and disappointment. Suter had suffered a third-degree ligament tear in the collision with Messier, not the most serious knee injury of all time, but one that would require six weeks of rehabilitation and a series of casts. By the time the last cast came off, the season was already over, the Stanley Cup already decided.

Nobody discovered Joel Otto. In some ways, that is hard to believe in retrospect. A six-foot-four, 220 pound centre, Otto should have been hard to miss — but twenty-one NHL teams found him easy to overlook. Otto came out of Bemidji State, a Division II school in northern Minnesota, that wasn't especially known for turning out pro prospects. Until Otto made it big, Bemidji, Minnesota was mostly known as the birthplace of Jane Russell. Otto put it on the map for something more seasonal. Following four years of college hockey that he completed in 1984, Otto engaged an agent, Brian Burke of Boston, who was asked to shop him around the NHL.

When Burke called the New Jersey Devils, they sounded interested. They were interested enough to offer Otto $750 to attend training camp. He would have to earn a contract. When Burke called the Philadelphia Flyers, they too invited him to camp. They didn't even offer $750. Otto was expected to go on his own, trying to catch the coaches' eyes. Other teams were willing to gamble as much as Philadelphia on Otto: no cash, just a chance to rise above the chaff in a few short days — or give up any thought of playing pro.

Finally, Burke called Flames' general manager Cliff Fletcher and convinced him to offer his client a contract. Fletcher acquiesced. The Flames paid Joel Otto the minor-league minimum to play for Moncton Golden Flames, their No. 1 affiliate.

For their largesse, Otto scored twenty-seven goals and sixty-three points in Moncton and won a share of the American League's rookie-of-the-year award. Otto came up for the final seventeen games of the 1984-85 season and showed Johnson something that not everybody else saw right away: that Otto, handled correctly, could do for the Flames what giant left winger Tim Kerr did for the Philadelphia Flyers.

The similarities between the two were clear. Like Kerr, Otto represented a large presence in front of the opponent's goal. Like Kerr, Otto scored at every level he played at. Like Kerr, Otto was a late bloomer who wasn't drafted. He signed as a free agent. Unlike Kerr, however, Otto wasn't terrorizing goaltenders.

In the first twenty-seven games of the 1985-86 season, Otto did everything the team asked of him — defensively. Johnson used him on the power-play. He used him to shadow the opposition's top centre. He used him as a face-off man. Otto saw a lot of ice time. For all that, he scored only two goals in the first third of the season.

Johnson's reasoning behind his use of Otto was understandable. He could afford to be patient with a struggling, rookie centre when the rookie was big and strong and the team continued to win. The night Otto broke loose and matched his season's output by scoring two goals, the Flames were on a ten game home-ice, undefeated streak. They were tied for third overall with the Washington Capitals. They were also about to begin their record losing streak. Luckily, Otto — a giant Teddy Bear of a man — had earned a reprieve and a permanent place in the line-up. Not only did Otto end his scoring slump that night against the Los Angeles Kings, Johnson had also hit upon a defensive strategy that would guarantee Otto his place in the line-up the rest of the season. Johnson experimented by putting Otto out against the Kings' diminutive centre Marcel Dionne. With an eight-inch height advantage, Otto turned the prolific Dionne invisible. The move proved to be the start of something big for Otto. From that point on, Otto found himself playing against the opposing team's No. 1 centre almost all the time — against everybody from the six-foot-four Mario Lemieux to the five-eight Dionne. For a big man, Otto showed surprising foot speed. He could keep up. When his awe at being in the NHL finally stopped, he developed into the team's top defensive centre.

"It's funny," said Otto. "All through my career, starting in high school, I've always been a slow starter. As a sophomore in high school, as a freshman in college, I hardly played. Each year, I kept improving. I don't think I ever set any goals for myself. It's just the way things progressed in my life, in my career. Before, I was just happy to be here in the NHL. Now, I'm starting to feel I can be, if not a force, then at least someone who maintains his ground. I want to be more than just an average, filler-type player.... It's a big jump — even from Division II college to Division I. Up here, I find you can't make too many mistakes. Your passes need to be right there. You have to constantly move the puck. When I was in college, they would give me the puck and I brought it over the blueline and tried to make the play — hit somebody going to the net or something. Here, everybody's so good, you can't take the puck over the blueline by yourself, you've got to use everybody on the ice. You've got to move it to the upper man. That was an adjustment for me.''

"Can he be another Kerr? I can't answer that,'' said Johnson. "He needs to make another step. Plus, Kerr has a better shot. Otto has played well for us, but he hasn't done the things in games that I've seen him do in practice. He may never do them, I don't know. We can only hope the maturing process continues.''

It did. Like Suter, Otto made huge strides in the second half and then became one of the team's most important players in the playoffs. When the Vancouver Canucks scored two power-play goals against the Flames in one of the final regular season games, Johnson moved Otto onto the penalty-killing unit. He needed his skills as a face-off man. Against Edmonton, against St. Louis, against Montreal, Otto — the man Johnson likes to station near the crease — took more punishment from opposing defencemen than any other player on the Flames. He took a beating, but he never came out of the line-up.

"His mother and dad were here watching,'' said Johnson. "They must be wondering about the National Hockey League. It looked as if he'd been to war. It looked as if he'd spent ten

117

years in Vietnam. His whole body is bruised. One thing I
learned about Joel Otto in the playoffs is that he's a competitor.
When you get to the finals, you need people who can compete.''

Perry Berezan could identify with Joel Otto. In a rookie
season that started so promisingly, Berezan also looked as if
he'd been to war by the end of the campaign. Unlike the
majority of rookies who were trying to make the team in
training camp playing alongside other rookies, Berezan found
himself playing with Hakan Loob and Mike Eaves. Berezan
had played nine regular-season and two playoff games in the
1984-85 season after joining the Flames from the University
of North Dakota. Some players had to play their way on the
team. On the strength of Berezan's cameo appearance the year
before, the only way he wasn't going to make the team was if
he played himself off the roster. When Berezan signed his first
contract, he was suffering from both strep throat and blood
poisoning. Normally, his playing weight was around 190
pounds. By the time he recovered enough to play, Berezan
was down to 180. The only flaw in his game was a marked
tendency to get knocked off the puck. Over the summer,
Berezan was asked to improve his conditioning and increase
his strength. Johnson was already sold on his hockey sense. In
part because Johnson's system was similar to the system he
played in college, Berezan was able to fit in almost overnight.
In the season-opener, Berezan scored twice in the Flames' easy
win over the Winnipeg Jets. If he could play as effectively the
rest of the season, then Berezan would be a keeper.

Things started to go sour for Berezan soon afterwards. As
the Flames completed their first extended road trip with a mid-
November loss to the Buffalo Sabres, Berezan didn't come

home with the team. Instead, he went to Rochester, Minnesota, home of the Mayo Clinic. Berezan couldn't understand why his ears plugged up whenever he exercised, something that prevented him from breathing properly. The club doctors couldn't find anything medically wrong with him so they decided to let someone else to to work on him. Berezan went through eight tests in a single day and found that he was basically healthy. However, they discovered that the tubes in his ears plugged up when he worked up a sweat, causing him to lose carbon dioxide out of his lungs. They prescribed some pills and eventually the problem went away.

Around then, the Flames decided to experiment with Berezan by turning him into a right winger. With Dan Quinn, Carey Wilson, Doug Risebrough, and Otto, the Flames were solid down the middle. They wanted more depth on the right side. So Berezan made the move, the first time in his career that he'd played a position other than centre. Berezan found he had to think things out more. Centre came naturally to him. On right wing, he had to concentrate more on his positioning, especially in his own zone. The net result of too much thinking and not enough reacting was becoming evident in his play. He had scored as many goals in the last seven weeks as he did on opening night: exactly two.

Then, just as he started becoming more relaxed in his new position, Berezan came down with the flu. Not a twenty-four hour, garden-variety bug, but a lengthy, taxing case of influenza. That cost him six more games. Berezan looked like a pale-faced clone of Banquo's ghost as the Flames tiptoed through the latter part of January. As was the case the previous year, the minute the Flames began losing players to injury, they suddenly started winning. With defenceman Paul Reinhart filling in on right wing, Berezan was finding it difficult to get back into the line-up. ''You wonder sometimes,'' said Berezan. ''The team was winning. Do they want to break up a winning line-up? Everybody was playing pretty good. Do they wait until they lose a game before they put you back in?... You start to wonder what your role is.''

The matter of Berezan's role in the overall scheme of things wasn't even clear to Johnson. Would Berezan be a scorer? Or a defensive player? A playmaker? Or a utility player? ''It's funny,'' said Berezan. ''When we were getting our report cards, C.J. (coach Johnson) asked me almost the same questions. First we talked about my goal production. He saw I only had eight. He thought that was pretty low. Then he looked at my shots on goal and said I must be getting chances. The thing is, I've never really been a top goalscorer. I always put my two cents in and at the end of the year, my totals would be there. If you're asking me, am I happy with my goal production, the answer is no. I'm not happy with it at all. I can look back and remember so many chances I've had to score. But you can only go so long with just getting chances. You can't be happy with that alone. You've got to start putting the puck in the net.''

Berezan eventually found the range for another four goals before the third week of March and a third catastrophe in a hard-knock kind of year. Berezan suffered a nondisplaced fibular fracture of his left leg in a game against Minnesota North Stars. The first report indicated he would be out for the season. The second day's news was considerably better. Berezan had suffered a small break about five inches above his left ankle. Doctors put a cast on it and told him to cross his fingers. The Flames needed to get to the second round before he could conceivably return to the line-up. The culmination of all his bad luck would have been enough to drive a different player to pack it in for the season. Not the effervescent Berezan. ''I could really go into the depression tank if I thought about it, so I'm keeping a positive attitude,'' said Berezan. 'I'm going to Winnipeg. I'm going to work out every day. I want to keep myself involved. If I stop hoping, stop trying, then I know I'm never going to get back.''

To keep Berezan's cardiovascular capacity up, trainer Jim (Bearcat) Murray modified a stationary bicycle so the twenty-one-year-old rookie could pedal it with his hands. The cast on his leg didn't stop Berezan from weight training either. Five-and-a-half weeks later, with Carey Wilson sidelined because of a lost spleen, Berezan was inserted into the line-up for a playoff game against the Edmonton Oilers. He would only score one goal in the playoffs — the one goal that lifted the Flames over the Oilers in the seventh game of the Smythe Division final.

Justice for the kind of season he had? Perhaps. Berezan, the only Flames' player from the Edmonton area, couldn't stop talking that fateful night. ''It's something to put in the books and tell my grandchildren,'' he said. ''It doesn't matter how it went in... we dethroned the Stanley Cup champions. To me, living in Edmonton, I know how the Oilers and the Eskimos have given it to Calgary. I couldn't dream of it happening any better. It's something I'll never forget.''

9
St. Louis

"...We don't have a system. While they're out practising our system, we're out drinking Budweiser."

CHARLES BOURGEOIS, ST. LOUIS BLUES

In the vanilla-flavoured world of professional hockey rhetoric, Joey Mullen's passion was a refreshing change. Normally, he was such a quiet man, an athlete who treated a microphone as if it were the enemy, and a questioning reporter with silent disdain. He didn't expect to be in Calgary in May — and he didn't expect to be playing against his old team, the St. Louis Blues, least of all for a chance at the Stanley Cup. Mullen had felt badly used by Harry Ornest, the owner of the Blues, because Ornest would not budge an inch during the previous summer's contract negotiations, and because he had given Mullen verbal assurance that he wouldn't be traded to a Canadian team. Mullen's departure from St. Louis wasn't easy, not for him, not for his wife, not for the Blues. His former teammates made no attempt to hide their dissatisfaction when he was traded to the Flames. They showed their emotions in tears. Mullen left for Calgary; his pregnant wife, Linda, left for their off-season home in Boston. He moved out on his family, in with traded teammate Terry Johnson, and into Eddy

Beers' Calgary home. Life could not have been more unsettling. Except for the hockey. That was the pleasurable part.

When Mullen returned to the decrepit St. Louis Arena in late February, a few weeks after being traded, it was long before the Flames and Blues would meet in a match of consequence. Not knowing what the future would bring, this was his private Stanley Cup. He and Harry Ornest were the combatants. "Something to prove?" Mullen repeated at the time. "I said it on television when I left: I want to stick it to Harry Ornest." But right away, he found things different in St. Louis. He found out how fleeting fame could be. "I walked in the door today to come to practice and the guy at the gate says: 'Can I help you?' I told him I play for Calgary. This is a guy I've seen almost every day for the last five years. Unbelievable!"

Being the central figure in the mid-season trade, Mullen garnered more attention than he cared to deal with. He was soft-spoken, almost inaudible at times, except when the subject was Ornest. Then, there was fire in his eyes. Then, there was a raspiness in his combination New England-New York accent. Despite the early problems, the trade worked out well for Mullen. He easily fit in with the Flames, was quickly productive and eventually was awarded with a new, long-term contract with figures he never would have dreamed of attaining in St. Louis. Mullen wasn't alone in reaping the benefits of the trade. Of the three players the Flames sent to the Blues, the least expected became the most prominent: Charles Bourgeois.

With the Flames, Bourgeois spent more time in the press box than he ever did on the ice. His main role was to keep everyone happy. He was the resident comedian, the champion of the one-liner. He had the quote ready before the question was even asked. Bourgeois was a reporter's delight, except for one small factor — the Flames didn't think he could play. St. Louis coach Jacques Demers quickly found otherwise.

Bourgeois soon made his mark in St. Louis, both on the ice and off. When Bourgeois first arrived in St. Louis, he wasted little time making friends. On his first television appearance he was asked how he was adjusting to the deal. Bourgeois said it was easier for his cohorts in the trade, Beers and Gino Cavallini, because Beers was married and Cavallini had his girlfriend with him. He said he was just a lonely single guy, living at a St. Louis hotel. He happened to mention the name of the hotel, and when he arrived in his room later that night, there were numerous messages, telegrams and flowers. Bourgeois was St. Louis' newest matinee idol. Sort of.

When Bourgeois arrived in Calgary for Game 1 of the Campbell Conference final, he didn't want to stick anything to anybody. Except perhaps a joke. "Is it true the scalpers were getting $500 a pair (Calgary-Edmonton series)," Bourgeois asked. "If they're getting $500 for this one, I'll be out there myself tonight."

He said the Blues needed the win more than the Flames did. "I've been to Lanny's (McDonald) house. I know the style he lives in."

The Blues had been accused, whimsically, of winning with mirrors. Coach Jacques Demers was dubbed Jacques DeMirrors. Bourgeois didn't deny the magic. "We're going to sneak into the rink before the game and put up the mirrors." It all sounded good, but the good humour lasted only until the first game of the series. After that, all jokes were put aside. The series had begun, more seriously for the Flames than they had ever imagined.

It was as if Demers had peeked into one of Bob Johnson's notebooks and stolen the secret formula. Everything the Flames had done successfully in beating the Oilers, the Blues had managed to do to win the opening game of the Conference final. They played it true to form: dull, simple, and slow. If the

Oiler series had the drama of an Ali-Frazier encounter, the first game of the series was more comparable to Ali-Wepner. "We're just a bunch of boring guys," Eddy Beers said after the Flames lost 3-2 at the Saddledome. "I think they'd better get used to it."

If the Flames had done anything wrong, other than fall into the obvious hypnotic trap the Blues had set in the opener, it was their failure to execute. Somehow, after Gary Suter had gone down in the final game of the Edmonton series, after Dan Quinn had been benched, after the Blues confused the Flames, the special teams fell apart. The Flames, from top to bottom, looked confused by the St. Louis system. They had had problems. "When I was with the Flames, we used to practise and this close to the Stanley Cup, they were again having problems. "When I was with the Flames, we used to practice using the St. Louis system, and then we would play them and lose," Charlie Bourgeois said. "And then the next day we would practise it again. And then I got traded here, and I found out we don't have a system. While they're out practising our system, we're out drinking Budweiser." The morning after the opening game loss, Bob Johnson sat behind his desk wondering what had gone wrong, talking again about the St. Louis system. The two coaches in the series already appeared to be playing a psyche game and Demers was playing it better. He was fostering the poor little Blues image, and selling it well.

Johnson was worried that Demers was selling the never-say-die Blues business too well, and because of it he began to envision his Stanley Cup dream slipping away. Johnson had been acting oddly in recent days, but with him the eccentricities are part of the package. He seemed to be doubting his chances for the first time. The normally positive Johnson didn't appear that positive at all. "Two of our key guys are in hospital," he said of Suter and Carey Wilson. "That takes away from our offence. We don't have anybody offensively who can do the job. It would be nice to have some extra forwards around.'' A few steps from Johnson's office, just a room away, centre Dan Quinn sat wondering what had gone wrong.

Johnson said the Flames didn't have any extra forwards, but there was Quinn, who had led the Flames in point production in the regular season, not dressing for the series opener. Quinn had become the forgotten man of 1986, the Kent Nilsson of years gone by, the player most likely to be benched. It used to be a role reserved for Steve Bozek, but Quinn had inherited it at playoff time. He had already been benched four times in the playoffs, more than any other Flames regular. ''Frustration has set in,'' said Quinn, the youngest Flame at age twenty, who had difficulty enjoying the victory over the Oilers because he had so little part in it. At one time, during the scenes of rejoicing in the Flames dressing room after the seventh game win over Edmonton, Quinn was seen with his head down, looking unhappy. Once, general manager Cliff Fletcher told him to lighten up. But Quinn was young, and having difficulty controlling his emotions. His team was winning, he wasn't, and that didn't make things any easier.

''Obviously, they don't think I can do the job,'' he said quietly. ''I don't think they think I can be an effective player. It was tough when Wilson went down. I figured I'd move back into the line-up. It's discouraging when you see two guys who haven't played centre all year playing your position in the playoffs. It's disappointing. You try to be a part of it, but it's difficult when you're not playing.'' With Quinn, Suter, and Wilson out, the Flames were missing one-third of their season's power-play goals. Changes had to be made, and Quinn was included in the line-up adjustments. He didn't know it then, but he was to become a significant factor in the series, primarily for his work on the power-play. His addition to the Flames' line-up was one of the predictable moves made by Johnson. When Quinn was added for Game 2 of the series, few paid much attention. Another addition captured all the attention then. A move few understood, even after it was explained.

Mike Eaves retired from professional hockey on October 18, 1985, ending a career which had been marred by head injuries. With one season remaining on his contract, the Flames did the honourable thing. They made him an assistant coach. Just what his responsibilities were, no one really knew. Bob Johnson handled the team. Bob Murdoch handled the defencemen. Pierre Page took care of the videotape. Glenn Hall worked with the goalies. Assistant coach Eaves practised with the team, just like any other player, but with no apparent function. He had retired before his time, a retirement imposed by a series of concussions which had plagued him. Yet, he stayed in condition. Before the playoffs began, Bob Johnson turned to him and said, ''Will you be ready if I need you?'' Eaves wasted no time in answering.

When he first appeared in uniform for the pre-game skate of a Smythe Division final game against the Oilers, most observers assumed it was a ploy by Johnson. Why dress a retired player for a pre-game warm-up? What sense could it possibly make? When asked about it, Johnson ducked the question, merely saying that Eaves was his ''edge''. Just what that meant at the time no one seemed to know. When Game 2 of the St. Louis series began, only one thing looked certain. Bob Johnson had finally snapped. Mike Eaves, who hadn't played a game for almost eight months, was dressed in what was then the Flames' most important game of the season.

He didn't worry about the ifs: the brain damage doctors had talked to him about, the chance to sound like Muhammad Ali in later life. Eaves considered all the facts and left one impression. He wanted his name on the Stanley Cup. This was his way of doing it. His return to the Flames line-up caused great debate. Members of management quietly second-guessed the coaching move. The fans were puzzled. It appeared to be the wrong move at the wrong time. Eaves played, and while not efficient enough to make a difference, the team played inspired hockey. The Flames were ready for Game 2, led by the not-ready-for-retirement line of Risebrough, McDonald, and Tonelli. Risebrough scored one of the few three-goal hat tricks of his career. The Flames won 8-2, and were headed to St. Louis looking to take back the home ice advantage they had lost in Game 1. Just a day after being distressed at losing to the Blues, the Flames had discovered the secret to beating them: score first.

Jacques Demers was fully aware of what his club was capable of, and what they weren't. As with Johnson after Game 1, Demers was concerned about the manner in which his club was thrashed in the second game. But he was home now, playing in an uncomfortable surrounding for visitors, in St. Louis summer heat — so unseasonable for hockey. Demers knew this was his chance. He knew he had to make it clear. The last thing he said when he left the Blues' dressing room prior to the game was "No dumb penalties, guys. No unnecessary penalties. Let's play it smart. Let's go." Demers' plea had fallen on deaf ears. Twenty seconds into Game 3, the Blues trailed 1-0. The game, won 5-3 by the Flames, was never again in doubt.

Having taken their first series lead, the mood of the Flames changed. Having soundly beaten the Blues twice in a row, there were quiet hints the Flames were on their way to the finale. All they had to do was beat the Blues two more times, and beat the 30 degrees C heat of St. Louis in May. Time would tell that neither was going to be easy. In Game 3 at the Arena, 175 pound Hakan Loob lost six pounds playing in the sweaty, smelly Arena. Just about everybody lost between five and ten pounds. The energy loss was so severe Bob Johnson did the un-Johnsonable. The man who lives by the theory that practice makes perfect, cancelled practice. While Johnson was making noise by his unlikely move at the rink, away from the Arena, one of the Flames' six owners was making noise all his own.

Once a season, usually in the playoffs, the Flames treat their office staff, doctors, and management people to a trip on the road with the club. This time it was St. Louis, hot St. Louis. The small gathering of Flames' supporters had made their way to the Arena for Game 3, only to find not everything to their liking. Some had been verbally abused. Some had beer spilled on them. Most had found it a most uncomfortable setting. The Arena is a well-designed relic of a building, which hasn't been kept up. Flames' goaltending consultant Glenn Hall, who used to miss training camps when he played because he always said he was home painting his barn, said if he had known the Arena was so run-down, he would have painted it himself. Cliff Fletcher, a former Blues' assistant general manager, called it a pigsty. Owner Norm Green, who along with several members of the Flames' contingent sat in the stands at the Arena, went one step further.

"The place is an embarrassment to the league," Green said. "People here are out of control. They're rude and abusive. I can see why people don't bring their family to the games. It's risky. If I lived here, I wouldn't bring my kids to games. I've been to Chicago Stadium. I've been to Madison Square Garden. I've never seen anything like this. This is a classy city. The people of St. Louis deserve better than this. If somebody (owner Ornest) was in the hockey business to stay, these problems would be solved. The fact that someone isn't spending money on security and cleaning means he's putting dollars in his own pocket.

Upon learning of Green's words, Ornest launched into a tirade of his own, but decided to keep most of it off the record. On the record he did say, "I don't respond to ignoramuses. I don't respond to a Johnny-come-lately who's nothing but rags to riches. That's what Norm Green is." The irony of the situation was that Green had been involved with the Flames long before Ornest purchased the Blues. Later in the playoffs, NHL president John Ziegler warned Green his comments were not considered appropriate. What Ziegler didn't say was that they were, for the most part, accurate. In the summer of 1986, St. Louis City Council voted to condemn The Arena in its current state.

By the time Green and Ornest had finished their infighting, the Flames had lost one battle. They wanted to wrap up the series in five games, but found that chore impossible. Frustrated by themselves, the Blues, and by some questionable refereeing, the Flames returned to Calgary with the two teams tied after four games of the Conference final. Going by Johnson's theory of beating the Oilers, the shorter the series would be, the better chance the Blues would have of winning. The Flames had lost Game 4, by a 5-2 score. The series was now a best-of-three.

It had begun as such a friendly series. Calgary and St. Louis. Old teammates, old friends, two generic line-ups lacking in animosity, lacking in rivalry. Then, Green and Ornest went at it verbally. Then, Gino Cavallini crushed Lanny McDonald into the boards in Game 3 almost knocking him silly. Then, Doug Wickenheiser found a new use for his stick in Game 4. He played dentist and removed one of Mullen's teeth. Suddenly, with the prospect of a berth in the Stanley Cup final drawing ever closer, the post-season had turned into the mean season for both the Flames and the Blues. There was too much at stake for both clubs, and too little time left. Calgary had little trouble winning Game 5 at home. The role players of the Flames finally out role-played the Blues. St. Louis had been winning in the series with big performances from small names. The Flames, led by Steve Bozek, out-blued the Blues to go ahead again. The next day, the Flames left for St. Louis, figuring their trip to the Stanley Cup final was just one game away.

Jamie Macoun heard a shout, and the rest was just a blur. A freeze frame of panic. He had heard a voice he thought was Allan MacInnis's. He thought he heard the instructions properly. He thought he knew what to do. Before he even had decided what to do, he had made the wrong decision. St. Louis had scored an emotional tying goal. Unbelievably, Game 6 was going into overtime.

The quiet celebration hadn't actually started on the Flames bench, but some were thinking about it. Calgary led by three goals with just over five minutes left to play. But quickly, the 5-2 Flames lead appeared in doubt. First Greg Paslawski scored, then Brian Sutter scored, and the Flames were doing everything, it seemed, to hang on. They weren't getting much help from a shaky Mike Vernon in goal. Not when they needed it most. And then it happened. Vernon went behind the goal to stop an angling puck. He nudged the puck to Macoun, who turned up towards the Flames goal with so many options. He could have banked it off the boards. He could have flipped it out of the Flames' zone. He could have headmanned it up ice. Instead, he did nothing. Had it been anyone but Macoun, it may have been of concern to the coaches. But it was Macoun. The same Macoun who had been falling out of trees head first and landing on his feet ever since he joined the Flames. When the large defenceman first left Ohio State to become a Flame, his penchant was to make mistakes and quickly recover from them. He was amazing at it, really. As quickly as he would give a puck away, he would dive and get it back. He could have been voted most likely to recover. But not this time. This time Macoun fell out of the tree and landed on his head.

Somehow, some way, Paslawski had stolen the puck from Macoun's stick and in one motion scored the tying goal. Vernon never did have time to return to the net. And the night he lost his composure didn't end there. On a steamy night at the Arena, the Flames and Blues were going into overtime. The message to the Flames was heard with a loud clang. This wasn't their night.

Joey Mullen, wanting to stick it to Harry Ornest as advertised, bounced a slapshot off the crossbar just minutes into overtime. The puck had beaten goaltender Rick Wamsley. It did everything except advance the Flames into the final. And when Doug Wickenheiser scored in overtime a few minutes later, that premise was now in doubt more than ever before.

The silence in the Flames' dressing room was so overwhelming afterwards you could have heard a pennant drop. There were tears in some players' eyes, disbelief in others. They had choked away a victory and they knew it, not knowing if that would be their final opportunity. So many words could be used to describe the loss that night in St. Louis. But the most appropriate was still choke. In a game they had to win, they didn't. In a game they had control of, they lost control of themselves. Somewhere their playoff discipline had disappeared. The Flames left St. Louis that night by charter airplane, a long, quiet, four-hour flight; a reminder of what had just transpired, of what they had just let slip away.

Of all the concerns Bob Johnson had going into Game 7, his biggest worry was Mike Vernon. Vernon had been so strong against Winnipeg, so strong against Edmonton, but it seemed the longer this series progressed, the more he came under question. Was it now time for a change? Could Johnson afford to make the switch now? Could he afford not to? In truth, the decision was out of his hands. He had to go with Vernon. And he was worried about that. He didn't know how Vernon would react to his next start, or how his club would react after letting the series slip away. Not a funny man, Johnson even tried his hand at humour. "Is Glenn Hall around?" he asked of the retired Hall of Famer. "Maybe he can play tomorrow?"

As much as the Flames were worried about their goaltending, the Blues had finally solved their dilemma. Throughout two rounds of the playoffs, Greg Millen had done much of the netminding for the Blues — and he had done it well. It was Millen's acrobatics which enabled the Blues to beat Minnesota out in the opening round. And against the surprisingly tough Maple Leafs in Round 2, Millen stood out. Then, the series with the Flames started and Demers chose history over current history. He started Rick Wamsley in Game 1 of the series, only because of a 10-2 won-loss record against the Flames. Wamsley was strong in Game 1, then not so strong in Game 2. Millen started Game 3, and it looked as though Demers had made a mistake. Millen's style of over-challenging played right into the hands of the Flames' veteran shooters. With just slight hesitation, he seemed beatable. So Millen, the Blues' No. 1 goalie was on the bench. Wamsley, the No. 2 man, was starting. The final game match-up loomed as a battle between a sharp Wamsley and a dubious Vernon.

The Flames, who had earned so much respect for their discipline in the Edmonton series, were now being chastised for the lack of discipline in the Blues' series. After the Montreal Canadiens had advanced to the finals, there seemed two schools of thought in the hockey world. One was that an all-Canadian final, the first since 1967, would do wonders for the league and for the Canadian hockey fan. On the other side, there were those who thought a final between the Canadiens and the ex-Canadiens would be good for the league and hockey in St. Louis, which was still fighting for support. Ron Caron, the Blues' general-manager, had scouted many of the Canadiens players when he was head scout in Montreal. Wamsley was a former Hab, so was Wickenheiser, Paslawski, Mark Hunter, Ron Flockhart, Ric Nattress, and Rick Meagher. There seemed history in the rivalry. There was no Flames-Canadiens history. Two nights before the final game, the scoreboard at the St. Louis Arena lit up brightly: "Stanley Cup championships, Game 1, Friday." The Flames were making no similar promises.

Doing the only thing he could have done, Bob Johnson started Mike Vernon in the seventh game of the Conference final. He was apprehensive about it, and in time it appeared so were the Flames' players. They came out with just one plan in mind: keep the puck out of their own zone. They played the game almost to perfection. Fitting neatly in size-nine Cinderella slippers, Vernon won for the eleventh time in the playoffs, stopping seventeen of the eighteen shots he saw in a 2-1 win by the Flames. The Flames had won the previous series on a goal which had been described by some as divine intervention. There was no such intervention on the night of the final game. They borrowed a page from the St. Louis playbook and won the series by playing blue collar hockey. Colin Patterson, a defensive star in the Edmonton series and an offensive star in the St. Louis series, scored Calgary's first goal. A blue-collar player had scored the biggest goal of a blue collar series. When Al MacInnis scored to make it 2-0, only one question remained: could Calgary hang on? Proving that Jacques Demers was right and boring can be beautiful, the Flames left the ice to a standing ovation, winners of the Campbell Conference, on their way to their first Stanley Cup final.

Doug Risebrough was handed the Clarence Campbell Cup by Scotty Morrison, and quickly his co-captains Lanny McDonald and Jim Peplinski were there to assist in hoisting up the Flames' newest jewel. The team celebrated on Wednesday night. By Thursday, they were preparing for a Friday game against the Canadiens. There was little time to enjoy the festivities. Little time to heal any hurts. The Stanley Cup final was set to begin. The loser had already been determined. But the Flames didn't know it then. It would take several days before they would realize what really had happened.

When they lost the sixth game in St. Louis, they had lost their preparation time, they had lost their resting time. In the smoldering heat of a St. Louis night, the Calgary Flames melted and lost the Stanley Cup. They just didn't know it then.

10
The All-Canadian Final

"The playoffs are a marathon. Sometimes you've got to stop for water along the way."   BOB JOHNSON

Outside the dressing room door, down the hall from the wild victory celebration, Lanny McDonald stood — his hair matted by perspiration, his eyes starting to water — waiting for the television interviewer, John Davidson, to get his cue. As the seconds passed and the emptiness started to sink in, McDonald excused himself and ducked into the dressing room for a towel. The moment gave him a chance to compose himself and when he went on national television, the tremble in his voice was the only visible clue to what had just happened. This wasn't the way McDonald's dream — of the Flames' so-called Run For One — was supposed to end. In a perfect world, the thirty-three-year-old right winger, playing in what could have well been his first and only Stanley Cup final, was supposed to skate around the ice, with the Stanley Cup held aloft. He was supposed to get the ultimate reward back for all the years he put in. It didn't happen. The Flames had overcome the largest stumbling block of all, the Edmonton Oilers, only to see themselves overcome by a Montreal Canadiens' team that they matched up so well against. On paper anyway.

The disappointment of coming so close and then not winning it all deeply affected the popular McDonald. So much of his identity is tied up in the bristly moustache and the Flaming C. When the Flames' last rally in the fifth game came up one goal short, McDonald tried to hold back the tears and simply could not. McDonald talked about the disappointment and tried to tell himself that it wasn't the end of the world, but no one was convinced.

The first all-Canadian Stanley Cup final in nineteen years began as a bookie's nightmare — the ultimate pick 'em series. Their styles differed, but the Flames and Canadiens were almost mirror images of each other in terms of their personnel and their cumulative records. In the 1984-85 season, the two teams finished in a dead heat for fifth overall in the NHL's composite standings. In the 1985-86 season, on the strength of three consecutive wins at the end of the regular season, the Flames edged the Canadiens for sixth overall and the home-ice advantage in the Stanley Cup final. Montreal finished seventh.

Moreover, the Flames' approach to doing business was the same as the Canadiens'. General manager Cliff Fletcher began his career in the Montreal organization in the 1960's, before joining the Flames' organization in 1972. When he moved with the team from Atlanta to Calgary and found himself with a sizably increased budget, he modelled the revamped Flames' franchise after the legendary Canadiens' teams that Sam Pollock built. The similarities didn't end there either. Both teams were relying on rookie goaltenders. Both recruited heavily from U.S. colleges. Both excelled on special teams. Both possessed good dressing-room leadership. Both teams' Stanley Cup heroes — Patrick Roy, Claude Lemieux, Mike Vernon — were barely household names in their own households prior to the playoffs.

The only significant difference was in the way they approached the game. The Canadiens relied on their defence: the rejuvenated Larry Robinson, the steady Rick Green, the improving sophomore Chris Chelios, the underrated Craig Ludwig. In the first fifteen playoff games, no team had put more than three goals past Canadiens' goaltender Patrick Roy in a game. The only time the Canadiens gave up more than three goals against, the Hartford Whalers put the fourth into the empty net in a 4-1 win over Montreal. Roy, who made forty-seven regular-season appearances, was *the* playoff story in the East. With an 11-4 record, a 1.77 goals-against average and a pleasing tendency to talk to his goalposts, Roy was the Canadiens' leading candidate for the Conn Smythe Trophy to that point.

By contrast, the Flames were solid, but not spectacular on defence. Without Gary Suter, the strongest part of their game was the ability to score goals. For two years running, they were the second-highest scoring team in the regular season behind Edmonton. In the playoffs, they had almost a dozen players dotting the Top 25 in scoring. Their test, as everybody saw it, was to get behind the Canadiens' defence so they could get to Roy. The first and only time Roy faced Calgary in regular season play at the Olympic Saddledome, the Flames found him vulnerable. They knocked him out of the game with four goals on eighteen shots in twenty-nine minutes. Since then, Roy had been nothing short of sensational. His numbers and his cool between the pipes reminded people of another time and another place — when a rookie named Ken Dryden led the Canadiens to an unexpected Stanley Cup championship fifteen years before. Roy didn't approve of the comparison. He thought the game had changed since Dryden's era. He thought that Dryden's goaltending had stood the test of time, that he was just a first-year player. Finally, Roy recognized how important his defencemen were to his gaudy statistics. ''Without them, I am nothing,'' said Roy.

The similarities between the teams and their recent history of close games convinced the players on both teams that they could pull it off. When Edmonton, the Philadelphia Flyers, and the Washington Capitals, the three top teams in the league, were eliminated before the semifinals, that threw the Stanley Cup wide open. Canadiens' left winger Mats Naslund decided, ''The Stanley Cup is more open than it has been in maybe the last fifty years. When you look at the teams which have already been eliminated, why wouldn't anybody want to give 150 per cent to win? Let's put it this way: every team starts a season with the idea of winning the Stanley Cup. But there are so many good teams around, it's becoming more and more difficult to stay alive in the playoffs. This season, with all the upsets, we could be closer to the Stanley Cup than we'll be in a long, long time.''

Canadiens' centre Bobby Smith made it clear the Flames hadn't cornered the market in terms of motivation either. In 1981, Smith — then a member of the Minnesota North Stars — helped end the Flames' first real playoff run. The 1981 playoff represented the one and only time Stanley Cup fever ran especially high in Calgary. That year, the North Stars eliminated the Flames and in turn, lost to the New York Islanders in the finals. Now, five years later, the twenty-eight-year-old Smith, older, wiser, smarter, was back playing for a championship. Recalling the North Stars' trip to the finals, Smith commented: ''We were really young then. We were a team that thought it was on its way to the top. We made it to the semifinals the year before, stopping the Canadiens who were trying for their fifth Stanley Cup. The next year, we were in the finals. We thought we were going to have that kind of playoff success every year — that if we didn't win it this year, we'd win it next year. Nobody had ever been to the Stanley Cup final before.

"This year is different. We have players who've won the Stanley Cup several times. We realize what a difficult road it is to get here. We are perfectly cognizant of the fact that we could enter the playoffs with a better team next year and lose in the first round. We realize this is a great chance for most of us to win our first Stanley Cup and for a couple of guys to win their fifth. We will be giving it our best shot."

Because the Canadiens eliminated the New York Rangers in five games, they had had a full week off between games. By contrast, the Flames — extended to seven games by the St. Louis Blues — had forty-eight hours to prepare.

Against that backdrop, the curtain dropped on Game 1 in Calgary, It took the Flames exactly one game to do what no other team could do in the playoffs: they solved the mystery of Patrick Roy. Two goals in a span of seventy-nine seconds early in the third period gave the Flames a 5-2 win over the Habs and a 1-0 lead in the series. Roy's impressive streak of holding the opposition to three goals or less in the playoffs came to a sudden halt as the Flames, using another generic effort, received goals from five different players to register the win. Jim Peplinski's controversial first-period goal put the Flames ahead to stay, but Dan Quinn's shorthanded goal 2:14 into the third was the winner. Ironically, Quinn was on the ice only because Steve Bozek, the team's regular penalty killer, was serving a minor penalty at the time. On the play, Quinn stole the puck from Canadiens' defenceman Chris Chelios and put a twenty-five foot slapshot behind Roy.

The Canadiens complained bitterly about Peplinski's goal, first, because it came with only nineteen seconds left in the first period; secondly, because they argued Peplinski knocked it in with a high stick. Referee Kerry Fraser ruled the goal was legal.

Roy didn't agree. He raced after the linesmen and pushed both of them. Fraser was within his rights to throw Roy out of the game. The league was within its rights to suspend Roy for his actions. All Roy received was a ten minute misconduct.

When the damage from the first game was assessed, two things became clear. Vernon was prepared to give Roy a run for the Conn Smythe Trophy. Canadiens' coach Jean Perron— like so many opposing coaches had before him — complained about the Flames' tactics. Vernon, the lesser known of the two rookie goaltenders, didn't possess Roy's sparkling numbers or his celebrated eccentricities — he wasn't talking to his goalposts in either of Canada's official languages — but he was just as anxious to win three more games for the Flames. Vernon outdueled Roy in the opener, especially in the second period, but he wasn't about to crow over his play. ''Management looks for performance,'' said Vernon. ''You have one bad year and you're going to find yourself down the ladder. That's where I found myself. You can prove yourself last night, okay fine, but what about tomorrow? You have to go out and prove yourself all over again. You can't just stop. You've got to keep going. That's what this game is all about. You have to keep proving yourself over and over.''

As Vernon retold his life story for the tenth time in the playoffs, Canadiens' coach Jean Perron was doing his best to inject some controversy into the final. Perron criticized the Flames for their ''interfering'' style, saying that it took away from the game. ''This is not classic hockey,'' said Perron. ''It's not right to see hockey taking this trend. We don't want to evolve into that.'' The Flames sacrificed finesse for muscle in the first game and the line of Jim Pepliski, Nick Fotiu and Tim Hunter ran roughshod over the Canadiens. Perron promised it would be different next time out.

It was. If the Flames won the opener because of Peplinski's

disputed goal, the Canadiens won the second game when Chris Nilan blocked Vernon out of the crease, allowing Gaston Gingras to score a goal into a wide-open Calgary net. Gingras' goal started a rally that eventually led to the Canadiens' 3-2 win — on Brian Skrudland's goal nine seconds into overtime. If Perron was upset with the Flames' semi-legal, hooking-and-holding style in Game 1, then Flames' coach Bob Johnson unloaded on the Canadiens following Game 2. Johnson accused the Canadiens and especially Nilan of trying to intimidate Vernon. ''They ran into him eight times,'' said Johnson. ''That Nilan's a real pro at it. He does it all the time. He's good at it. It's an intentional move on their part all night. How they have the nerve to say we interfere when they do something like that? It's a deliberately planned part of their attack.''

Despite the fact that Game 2 was decided in overtime, the Flames stayed close only because of Vernon. Robinson called Vernon a ''backstop in there'' as he held onto the one-goal lead until a third-period breakdown — the Flames were caught on a line change — led to the tying goal by Canadiens' rookie David Maley. Nilan hit the post twice in the second last minute. Otherwise, Montreal would have won in regulation. Clearly, Vernon wasn't as superstitious as Roy, who talked to his posts on the grounds that they'd come to his aid when a shot beat him. Not Vernon. Even if the posts were helping him out, he didn't plan on getting into any fireside chats with them.

With the series adjourning to less friendly and familar goalposts for the third game, the Canadiens thought the edge in the series had shifted to them. Their playoff record in the Forum was 8-1. For their part, the Flames thought a respectable 5-3 road record, including three wins in Edmonton's Northlands Coliseum, would stand them in good stead. They also hadn't lost two games in a row since the playoffs started. The series was tied 1-1. There was no reason to think this would be any different from the Oilers' series or the Blues' series. It had marathon written all over it.

The only nagging doubt in Johnson's mind was that his team could be running out of gas. Playing for the twentieth time in forty-one days, Johnson thought the gruelling playoff grind was taking its toll. Among the regulars, Johnson said the bruised and slumping Joel Otto along with Steve Bozek and Hakan Loob all needed a night off. Otto hadn't scored in eleven games. Bozek and Loob didn't get a shot on goal in the second game. Johnson hinted that he would put the team's newest recruit, rookie right winger Brett Hull, into the line-up for the third game. Hull, a sixth-round choice in the 1984 draft, joined the Flames during the St. Louis series following a distinguished two-year career at the University of Minnesota at Duluth. The Flames tried to sign him some months before, but Hull balked at their overtures. He wanted to play for team U.S.A. in the world championships. That experience, thought Hull, would help him decide if he was ready for the pros — or if he needed another year of college experience. Hull led Team U.S.A. in scoring. When he returned from the world championships, Hull gave the Flames his answer. He was ready.

When Game 3 began, Johnson surprised even his own team with the extent of his moves. He took out Bozek, Colin Patterson, Mike Eaves, and Paul Baxter. He put in three rookies — Hull, minor-leaguer Yves Courteau and Perry Berezan — as well as defenceman Terry Johnson. Patterson, one of the stars of the St. Louis series, came out of the line-up because of a worsening case of the flu. The other changes smacked of Johnson's desire to keep everybody — his team, the opposing team — a little off balance. You really couldn't tell the players without a program.

In the end, the changes didn't cost the Flames the pivotal third game. The timing of Montreal's scoring did. First, the Flames lost all their poise in a disastrous sixty-eight second span of the opening period when the Canadiens scored three times and turned a 2-1 deficit into a 4-2 lead. Then, after the Flames had slowly battled back into the game, they allowed the Canadiens' rookie Kjell Dahlin to score his first of the series and second of the playoffs with thirty-eight seconds remaining in the second period. Much as they did in the sixth game against St. Louis, the Flames inexplicably collapsed for a short time, but it was time enough for them to lose the game. The flurry began when Bobby Smith scored on a tip-in with only a minute and thirty-five seconds left before the intermission. With only forty-two seconds remaining, Naslund scored a power-play goal with Flames' defenceman Robin Bartel — who was in the line-up, replacing the injured Suter — off for holding. When Canadiens' right winger Bob Gainey put a screened shot past Vernon from thirty-five feet seconds later, that essentially did it for the Flames. Johnson signalled for Reggie Lemelin and when play stopped seventeen seconds later during an altercation, the Flames' coach changed goaltenders. For the first time since the finals began, Vernon had looked vulnerable. He wasn't happy about it either. Vernon stormed off the ice when Johnson took him out of the game. ''That's in my blood,'' said Vernon. ''When you get pulled, you get mad. I don't think I played a bad game. If you tell me I played a bad game, I disagree with that. The coach said: 'Good game Mike. It's not your fault.' Now we have to look ahead.''

Complicating matters for the Flames was the fact that they lost right winger Joey Mullen with a neck injury the same night. Mullen left the game in the first period when Gingras, the Canadiens' defenceman, ran him into the boards head first. The preliminary report indicated only a stiff neck. Mullen didn't even go to hospital. He decided he would sleep on it. He had forty-eight hours to recover. One day later, Mullen didn't look much better. With his head listing to one side, Mullen gingerly dragged himself across the hotel lobby and said maybe yes, maybe no. He just couldn't say if he'd recover in time to play the all-important fourth game.

With Mullen questionable and Patterson out, the Flames' ever-dwindling supply of players was becoming an acute shortage. Compounding the problem was the NHL's decision to crack down on the pushing and shoving that took place seemingly after every whistle. In Games 2 and 3, referees Andy van Hellemond and Don Koharski handed out ten misconducts, five to each team, to players who were wasting time. Invariably, the Flames lost out in every exchange. Their already depleted corps of defencemen cooled their heels three times for ten minutes apiece. Twice Neil Sheehy was found guilty. The Flames simply couldn't afford to go with a five-man rotation for too long. It put too much of a strain on an already overworked crew.

So the Flames' players questioned the officiating and they questioned the Canadiens' tactics and they even questioned the differences in the benches at the Forum. In short, they did everything they could to distract themselves from the fact that they would be playing the most important game of the season with a couple of important cylinders missing from the line-up. Just how much of a difference the ill and infirm would have made to the Flames wasn't ever made clear. Mullen took the warm-up with a cervical collar around his neck, but he determined that he couldn't play. By now, Patterson was so sick from an allergic reaction to penicillin that he was in hospital, on intravenous and out for the season. Even so, the Flames and Canadiens battled through more than fifty-one minutes of scoreless hockey before disaster struck. In trying to clear the puck out of the Flames' zone, Doug Risebrough inadvertently put a pass right on the stick of Canadiens' rookie right winger Claude Lemieux. Lemieux took two steps, wound up and put a hard slapshot between Vernon's legs. Lemieux's goal held up for a 1-0 Canadiens' win and a 3-1 stranglehold lead on the series.

No one in the Flames' dressing room wanted to talk about precedent, but then that was understandable. Precedent wasn't on their side. Nor was momentum, nor injuries, nor depth. Only two teams in playoff history had ever come back from a 3-1 deficit to win a series. Only once — the 1942 Toronto Maple Leafs — did a team ever do it in a Stanley Cup final. That Risebrough made the error that cost the Flames the game was the ultimate irony. Their frustration spilled out at game's end when the teams came off the benches and started an old-fashioned on-ice brawl that took more than fifteen minutes to tidy up. With Nilan directing the Habs' attack from the Montreal bench, with Lemieux biting Peplinski's right thumb, with Risebrough taking on his close friend Bob Gainey, the melee turned what had been a classic, old-school hockey game into a sideshow. Understandable, maybe. Undesirable, clearly. Within twenty-four hours, NHL president John Ziegler had slapped the wrists of both teams, handing out a total of $42,000 in fines. Fletcher and Serge Savard, the respective general managers, did a routine amount of complaining about the severity of the fines, but their hearts weren't really in it. Savard's team was a win away from the Stanley Cup.

With the series shifting back to Calgary, Fletcher's team had a more immediate goal in Game 5. This would be their record twenty-second playoff game of the season. All they wanted to do was force a record twenty-third playoff game. So when the subject of fatigue came up prior to the game, the answers were fairly predictable. What fatigue? Who's tired?

Not the Flames. When the end came — as it did that Saturday night in a 4-3 loss — no one on the Flames talked about climbing the mountain. They were only thinking about skiing down it. Indeed, none of the analogies used by the Flames in their Cinderella season sounded right that night. As Peplinski explained: "That's as close as I came in six years and that may be as close as I come for another six years. I don't want to think about next year. I've got six months to think about next year. I wanted to carry the Cup around the ice."

In time, the Flames were able to reflect on what a remarkably successful season they had had, but on the last weekend in May, all they could think of was how close they came and how long it may take them to go that far again. The Flames didn't go without a struggle. They started to close a 4-1 deficit on Bozek's second goal of the game with four minutes remaining. They moved to within one on Joey Mullen's twelfth of the playoffs, a team record, with Vernon already out of the goal. They came within one shot — Jamie Macoun's from the edge of the crease with fourteen seconds remaining — of forcing overtime. But Roy smothered the puck and with it, the Flames' last chance of extending the series.

For the third time in four games, the Flames came up one goal short of the Canadiens. With the hockey season ending and the golf season beginning, Bozek finally acknowledged what everybody had been saying all along: the Flames simply didn't have enough left for the Canadiens. Simple as that, really. They gave it a shot but they didn't, they couldn't, give it their best shot.

"It's almost as if we were a step away the entire series," said Bozek. "We just weren't there. They played great defensively. We lacked the jump we had earlier on. I can't say if it was the culmination of the two seven-game series we played before, but there wasn't the sharpness we had before.

It seemed like the really, really hard-working goals weren't there. It wasn't a case of lack of effort. It was just a case of being worn down.''

''Playoff hockey is a strange bird,'' said Peplinski. ''The difference between winning and losing is very marginal — and the Canadiens had that margin.''

Inside the dressing room, across from Peplinski's stall, as the players began to filter out, McDonald was slowly regaining his composure. He started talking about the experience that he and his teammates went through. To McDonald, something had happened to this latest edition of the Calgary Flames, something magical, something that didn't happen every year to a pro team, something that may not happen again — even if it was the same team on paper. They will be one year older, one year wiser, one year different.

Said McDonald: ''I'm awfully proud of the character and composure this team showed through good times and bad. Once you get that feeling, you want it back again. We came a long way this year, a lot farther than the experts expected — but not the guys in the dressing room. They always felt we had a chance. Unfortunately, we didn't win it all this season, so we know we have to work that much harder next year.''

11
The C of Red

"And they said Calgary couldn't support an NHL team. Have we shown them, or what?" CLIFF FLETCHER

In the span of two months, they became something to everyone. To school teachers, attempting to finish a curriculum, they were a distraction. To provincial politicians looking for a smaller turn-out at the polls on election night, they were a bonus. To worried oilmen, who wondered how low the price of oil could go and how long before another set of layoffs would begin, they were a diversion. To sporting goods shops and souvenir stores, they were a financial bonanza. In the months of April and May, 1986, the Calgary Flames became the talk of the town. And they captured the attention of hockey fans everywhere.

In the span of two months, Calgary caught the fever — Flames fever. Radio stations took popular songs and Flamed them. Homes all across the city were draped with pennants and placards. A promotion urging Flames supporters to wear red clothing proved so successful that many Calgary stores actually ran out of red clothing. It wasn't just the fans at the Saddledome wearing red. People were wearing red in the banks and at gas stations and in schools. With a failing economy, the people of the city had nowhere else to turn; they turned to the Flames, for this was a special time.

So much had changed and so much had remained the same in the six years since the Flames had moved from Atlanta to Calgary. When the club first moved to the Stampede City, Calgary was still experiencing the last of the oil boom. People were louder then, more boisterous, more interested in the quality of their life than the quality of their city. The Flames arrived in rich Calgary at the right time. And because of it they were an easy sell.

Owner Nelson Skalbania had somehow outmanoeuvered a group of Calgarians bidding for the Flames and without using a penny of his own — creative financing, it's called — managed to secure the franchise from Atlanta owner Tom Cousins. Within a year, Skalbania had sold half interest, then his entire interest, back to the original group who bid for the franchise. He was in, then out, leaving the ownership to a quiet group of Calgarians led by the Seaman brothers, Doc and B.J., and businessmen Norm Green, Harley Hotchkiss, Ralph Scurfield, and Normie Kwong. In the fashion that made and lost Skalbania millions, he had left his mark on the club, a mark that wouldn't be noticed for many years to come.

When Skalbania first announced he had purchased the Flames, he made one mistake. He misjudged the people of Calgary. He misjudged the boom attitude. At the time, he whimsically remarked that season tickets would be available on the upcoming Monday, but if anyone was interested, they could drop their applications off on Friday, the day of the announcement. What Skalbania hadn't taken for granted was how much the people of Calgary wanted NHL hockey. In a matter of hours, the season tickets were oversubscribed — before they had ever officially gone on sale. On Monday morning, when the tickets were supposed to have been available to the public, the Flames, not a week old in Calgary, were in the midst of their first controversy. Too many applications; not enough tickets. It would take time to sort out, and it did. Because the team was moving into the Stampede Corral, a junior hockey building of 6,492 seats which would house an NHL team, tickets were at a premium. Eventually it was all sorted out. Some people got season tickets. Some got half season tickets. Some wound up with nothing. The Flames sold out that first season — and have sold out every regular season home game since. All by season ticket sales.

The rush for tickets resurfaced in their Stanley Cup season, when a few regular season ticket holders chose not to pick up their options on playoff seats. Suddenly, the Olympic Saddledome, the home of the Flames since 1983, became a campgrounds for people wanting Flames' tickets. Some slept outside for as long as two nights, some slept through snow, for the privilege of attending a Flames' game. It became something of a popular thing — camping out for Flames' tickets. But the race for tickets wasn't the only legacy Skalbania left behind.

A tradition began in the Flames' first year in Calgary, long faded into memory, by the time the club had made its way to the Stanley Cup final. The Flames club which had moved to Calgary was known for more than free spirits and size. They were known as a team which played well each season only to wilt each playoff. The assumption was the Flames of 1980-81 were no different, at least until they had proven different. Quickly, they proved to be nothing like their predecessors. They opened their playoff season with a three game sweep of the Chicago Black Hawks, ending when Willi Plett fired an off-wing slapshot past Tony Esposito in double overtime. That wasn't just a series win for the Flames. It was the first time

151

they had *ever* won a playoff series. After that, they played the Philadelphia Flyers, a team which finished higher in the standings — a team which was traditionally playoff tough. When the teams had split the first two games of the series, the Flames returned home, and were shocked to find a group of fans who made their way to the airport. It wasn't much, really, but it was something.

The Flames went ahead in the series and the Flyers battled back — but when Calgary lost Game 6 at home the feeling was the trip back to Philadelphia for a seventh game would be a waste of time. It turned out to be a waste of time for the Flyers, who were beaten. The Flames chartered across the continent, arrived home in the middle of a crazed night, and found Calgary airport jammed with supporters. The playoff hysteria began in earnest that night.

In between their first and sixth years in Calgary, the Flames had only the occasional playoff moment worthy of recall. There were the first-round wins over the Vancouver Canucks, but nothing else. Twice the Flames lost to the Oilers, once to the Jets, but they never advanced beyond the quarter-finals. And there were few mob scenes at the airport.

When Bob Johnson left the University of Wisconsin to become coach of the Flames, among his first observations was that the Calgary fans were too quiet. There was no atmosphere at Flames games, he said. There was noise at the Corral — the building lent itself to excitement — but the sterile, silent Saddledome was more theatre than arena and Johnson didn't like it. He tried to college-up the Saddledome. The Flames put up their own signs. It didn't work. They brought in a band. It didn't work. They brought in mascots. The mascots entertained when the hockey didn't. But it didn't liven up the crowd. They attempted to utilize their scoreboard to invoke spontaneity. But that approach didn't work either. So they tried a trumpeter and an organist and rock music and waves. Nothing worked. Calgary fans were simply unexcitable for all but four of the forty home regular season games. The four games against Edmonton. The rest they treated with silence more suited to a tennis match than a hockey game. They paid, they watched, they ate popcorn and they cheered at all the appropriate times. Only when the playoffs came, and when something was worth cheering about, did Flames fans act like fans.

In the Stanley Cup season, they were fanatical.

On the night his impossible dream ended against Montreal, Johnson stood behind the Flames bench, plotting what was to be the final minutes of his finest NHL season. He tried to concentrate, but could not. He glanced at his notebook, ran his hand over his contorted, expressive face. He heard noise — the noise he so often had asked for — but he didn't know what he was hearing. Johnson turned to his assistant coach, Bob Murdoch. There were two minutes left to play in their season. The Flames were buzzing. So were their fans. "What are they saying?" Johnson asked Murdoch. Murdoch paused for a moment to listen. "I think they're saying, 'Thank you, Flames'''.

Like an orchestra reaching for that final crescendo, the Saddledome fans had reached their finest moment at a time when the club they followed had so few moments left to go. The players were tired — the fans were not. They wanted more. When the whistles, cowbells, and trumpets fell silent on a final, fateful night, all that could be heard was the chanting of those dressed in red. As if it were planned, almost 17,000 people stood at once and began their near-religious refrain. "Thank You Flames. Thank You Flames." It carried on while the Flames scored to come within a goal. "Thank You Flames." It was heard as Flames players scrambled at Patrick

Roy's crease, trying to bang in a bouncing puck which would have sent the game to overtime. "Thank You Flames." It was heard as the Stanley Cup was presented to Bob Gainey. "Thank You Flames." They took their final bows and bid their fans goodbye. "Thank You Flames."

Johnson, who had previously wondered where the hockey spirit was, stopped wondering. In more than twenty years in his hockey life, never had he heard anything to compare to those final two minutes. "That was incredible," he would later say. He talked about it the night the Flames lost the Cup, the day after that — and the day after that. The fans touched their heroes, like they had never touched them before.

The Stanley Cup was won on a Saturday night and on Sunday the Flames rested. The club met Monday morning, for the last time in a season chock full of meetings. They listened for a few minutes, but mostly it was a post-season get-together. Pizza, beer, and have a good summer. Some players were going on holidays. Some were getting married. Some were going home to rest. Lanny McDonald sat at his locker for what seemed to be the longest time. Only a few players remained in the locker room and McDonald looked as though he didn't want to go. Most of the players took their fan mail and some personal belongings. But McDonald had too much mail to take. First, he passed around a wedding photograph someone had sent him. The picture was of a large wedding party, the men on one side, the women on the other, all holding up red McDonald moustaches under their noses. "I wish I knew who sent this," McDonald said. Then he showed his next gift. Someone had made him a lamp. Not an ordinary lamp, a hand-made lamp with a Flames shade and a hockey player holding it up. "This one is special," he said. He took another bite of pizza, another swig of beer, shook some hands and said goodbye. His eyes were the same colour as his road jersey.

While the Flames were saying their goodbyes, city council was meeting downtown. Plans were underway for Calgarians to get the opportunity to honour the Flames for their efforts. Normally, parades are reserved for champions, but this year was different. In Harford, the Whalers had been honoured by the city for their fine season. The city of Calgary wanted to do the same. In the hearts and minds of the people of Calgary, the Flames were their champions.

The Flames' wrap-up party went the night before the parade. Apparently, it claimed two victims. When the players were paraded down Ninth Avenue in a bright red firewagon, two regulars were missing. Goaltender Mike Vernon, the surprise story of the playoffs, wasn't there, nor was defenceman Jamie Macoun. The Flames said they knew Vernon and Macoun wouldn't be there. The fact is, both Vernon and Macoun overslept, missing the festivities. And the surprise was, no one really questioned it. People mobbed the streets to watch their favourites drive by, and few even noticed that two were missing.

Players, trainers, coaches, management, wives, and girl-friends waved as they were slowly driven to a podium on the Stampede Grounds. Estimates put the number of fans on the Grounds at 20,000 but it was difficult to tell. School children, not given the day off after a disagreement between city council and the school board, still attended. Mayor Ralph Klein had hoped the school board would have given children the day off to watch the Flames. The school board thought otherwise. The solution was simple. A lot of children came down with mysterious illnesses that day, all of which were hockey related.

The fans showed up, waving ''We're No. 1'' fingers, wearing red, carrying signs that paid tribute to the club which had led them on a Stanley Cup odyssey. ''We Want the Flames,'' one sign read. ''Next Year Is Our Year,'' read another. Many were wearing red McDonald moustaches.

Mayor Klein, both a people's champion himself and a Flames' fan, spoke to the gathering who came to support their club. "The twenty-six players on this team sparked a love affair," Klein bellowed. "I'm talking about a 100 per cent, get out of the way, full blown, stand back, love affair." The people shrieked. "A love affair between 600,000 people and one hockey team." The chanting began again.

Klein had long been a major backer of sport ventures in Calgary. The previous winter, he had fought to keep the football Stampeders in Calgary, despite city council's reluctance to do the same. And he used his opportunity at the Flames parade to remind the fans of his stand. "For those who feel there's no place for professional sports in this city, just look at what has happened here." Another cheer. "Just let me say thank you. Thank you Flames, for being a lightning rod for the pride we have always had in Calgary and the opportunity to express it once again." The banners waved, the fans chanted "Go Flames Go" and the players soaked up the sunlight.

Cliff Fletcher had always maintained a low profile in his job as the Flames' president and general manager, mostly because he chose to. Unlike his coach, he did not relish the spotlight. He chose to be businesslike, to remain in the background, to quietly get the job done. And quietly, he did it well, without interference from ownership. When Fletcher rose to follow Klein, few expected what they heard, a rousing speech, a tribute to both his club and its followers, delivered with a bravado Fletcher, at least publicly, had not been known for. Fletcher didn't speak often, but when he did it was usually effective. He spoke to the players once — during the Edmonton series. Once was enough.

"And they said Calgary couldn't support an NHL team,"

Fletcher said to the gathering at Stampede Park. "Have we shown them or what?"

"One thing I learned from reading the coaches horoscopes. They're better coaches in April and May than they were in December and January," Fletcher said, referring to the club's earlier slump. Then he turned serious.

"No one gave the effort the players did, right down until the final seconds the other night. The coaches said that they have never experienced anything in their lives in professional sports like you fans chanting 'Thank You Flames' in the last two minutes of the game.

"Our club will start next year with the inspiration you've given us this year.

"We have to prove we're No. 1. You fans have already proved you're the best sports fans in North America."

Slowly, after Lanny McDonald had spoken, after Bob Johnson had been presented with a Alberta championship trophy for beating the Oilers, after the last fan had chanted and the last autograph was signed, the celebration at Stampede Park broke up. The emotions of a city swirled, and so too did the emotions of the athletes on the Flames. In a span of two months, their lives had changed and so had their city. They were heroes before. Now, they had become legends.

The pictures of the Stanley Cup season are still so evident: Bob Johnson, wincing; Mike Vernon, with his arms in the air; Bearcat Murray, leaping behind the bench; Lanny McDonald, red faced and unshaven; Jim Peplinski, kissing the Campbell Cup; Doug Risebrough hugging Bob Gainey; Joel Otto, battered and bruised, limping out of the Flames' dressing room. They are pictures of victory and defeat, emotion and passion. They are pictures of a team — and its city. "Thank You Flames." The chanting didn't seem to slow. And then the season and the dream was over.

"If you're going to lose," said Flames' owner Norm Green, "it was a good way to go."

12
Looking Back At Glory

"We were given a chance, an experience of a lifetime."

MIKE EAVES

The Olympic Saddledome was silent in early June. The ice came out the day after the Flames had been eliminated. The only reminder of the past two months was found in the signs with Flames' logos which still hung from the balconies of the arena. So much had happened so quickly, and few knew how to react. In Edmonton, it had been more than a month since a hockey game was played at the Northlands Coliseum. The media tables, which had been arranged for the Stanley Cup final, were taken away after the loss to the Flames. The banner, declaring the Oilers as Smythe Division champions, was never used. For the Oilers, it turned out to be a summer they'd never forget — nor would they be allowed to forget it. For the Flames, their accomplishments proved unforgettable.

Bob Johnson tried to relax, but couldn't. Again and again, he played the Stanley Cup playoffs over in his mind. He smiled as he remembered John Tonelli's overtime pass to Lanny McDonald in Winnipeg, which enabled the Flames to win Round 1 of the playoffs. He remembered the pain of Gary

Suter and wondered how he could replace him. He remembered the final minutes of Game 6 in St. Louis, and what it all meant. He remembered it all. The hockey season had ended for his players, but Johnson couldn't stop thinking about the game which is his life.

Two days after the final game against Montreal, a jittery Johnson sat behind the desk in his office, his usual pre-game pose. He tried to talk about the season, about his club's success, but it was all too fresh in his mind. He hadn't removed himself from the final series. He was ready to play again, even if no one else was. "It was a funny wind down," Johnson said, months later. "I've never experienced anything like it before. We were playing, every other night, every other night, and finally when it was over, it wasn't over for me. I thought we were still playing. I just felt it and felt it. It wasn't like the Super Bowl. It wasn't a one-time shot. It was every other night and it seemed like it went on forever. It took a long while to get over it. You've set your pattern for a long time and it's not that easy to change. I was in a groove and it took a while to change that. I had trouble relaxing. It's over now, but it took me a while to do something different, to do something else. We played 113 hockey games in 249 nights. That's all we did. It was like being in a hockey vacuum."

Johnson took almost two months to put the season in its proper perspective. He played games over in his head and thought about the many decisions he had had to make. As he looked back, one moment struck him as more important than any other. It wasn't Steve Smith's error. It wasn't the seventh game victory over St. Louis. It wasn't the thrills of the parade, or the chanting of the Calgary fans. In retrospect, Johnson thought the most important moment of the playoffs came when McDonald's overtime goal knocked Winnipeg out of the playoffs. Johnson thought that McDonald's goal enabled the

Flames to have enough time to prepare for the Oilers. "When I look back, I don't know what would have happened had we lost that game in Winnipeg," said Johnson. "I don't think we would have been able to beat Edmonton. I don't think we would have been ready if we had to play another game or two. To me, that was the most important moment. To me, that was the difference."

Once the season ended, Johnson left Calgary for his summer hockey schools in the United States, thinking he had left the Flames behind. He found out he couldn't. Or wouldn't be allowed to. In eight weeks, a team which previously had few fans outside its own city, suddenly had built up a following. Johnson held up a newspaper clipping once during the playoffs, saying "they were writing about us in Tokyo." Even then, he wasn't totally aware of the impression the Calgary Flames had left.

Suddenly, after years of running hockey schools in places such as Aspen, Vail, and Colorado Springs, Johnson became something of a celebrity. From the time the Flames-Oilers series began, the Flames became the target of much of ESPN's television coverage in the U.S. ESPN's rating for hockey had never been higher, and the Flames and Oilers were their best attraction. Johnson knew the exposure was large, he just didn't know how large. Everywhere he went, people recognized him. The youngsters he had been teaching for years at hockey schools suddenly looked at him differently. "Little kids from Idaho or Nevada would come up to me and say 'Good playoff, coach' or 'Way to go, coach. You almost had them.' It seems everyone saw the Flames. Everywhere you go now, people know who the Calgary Flames are. It was funny the way it was. I got letters from all over and everywhere I went, people talked about the hockey. Now, there's a whole group of Flames' fans out there, who never even heard of us before."

Johnson didn't return to Calgary until early September, just a few weeks prior to the start of another training camp. He was again wound up to start the grind again, ready to repeat, even if the odds were against him. ''I can't be satisfied to talk about last year. I want to enjoy it again. I want to enjoy this year.'' He was ready to begin another season, with virtually the same line-up he almost won the Cup with.

Of all the questions which remained at season's end, one could never be properly answered. What would have happened had Steve Smith not scored in his own net? Would the Flames have beaten the Oilers? Would the Oilers have come back and won their third straight Stanley Cup? But these are questions that cannot be answered. Not by the Oilers, nor by the Flames. And not by the individuals most directly involved.

Like Bob Johnson, Steve Smith, the scapegoat of Oiler misfortune, also had difficulty relaxing in early summer. The question was still on his mind. It had to be. It would take weeks for everything to be straightened out in his head. The pass. The deflection off Grant Fuhr's leg. The buzzer which signified the end of the game. The teary answers he classily supplied to the interrogators who would brand him, perhaps wrongly, the cause for the end of a dynasty. Smith learned of his infamy. He was the guy who had scored the goal. He made the national news in two countries. He became an answer to a trivia question, and his unfortunate action would be seen on every sports blooper film from here to eternity. Smith would not be forgotten — and he knew it.

He wasted little time in leaving Edmonton when the Oiler season abruptly ended, but soon he found out how small the world had become. Standing outside his in-laws home in

London, Ontario, Smith was washing his blue Bronco when two young hockey fans walked by.

"That guy plays in the NHL," said one.

"Yeah, I know," said the other. "He's the guy who scored *the* goal."

Steve Smith could only laugh. It was the best of his options.

"The first couple of days (in Edmonton) it was tough to deal with," Smith told the *London Free Press* in an interview. "After that, you collect your thoughts and realize it's not the end of the world, that it's just another game. The whole team went out one night and the next night I just stayed home around the apartment and my wife took some calls. A lot of people from back home were calling. After that we unplugged the phone and I went for a walk in the park to collect my thoughts."

"You come to grips with it. It's not that bad a thing. Nobody shot anybody."

It wasn't such a bad thing, but it became a famous thing. Almost from the day the Oilers were eliminated in the playoffs, Smith's daily mail began increasing. The Oilers, with Gretzky, had seen this much mail before. But never for another player. At first, it was just a few letters. But it didn't stop. With two bags, Smith estimated he received more than 3,000 letters. And those were the ones he received at home. The Oilers received more. Entire school classes took it upon themselves to console Smith. Some sent him jokes. Some sent him invitations to social functions. Smith wanted to answer the letters, but could not. There were simply too many.

Of all the letters Smith received, he said there wasn't a single negative one. He took solace in the writing of fans. And some were printed in the *London Free Press* Saturday magazine.

Dear Steve:

I want you to know I'm sorry about your accident and that we all still love you for your great playing and everything. I'll tell you a joke, okay? Why didn't the skeliton go to the seinyour prom? Because he had nobody to dance with? Well, sorry again.

Love, S.H.

Dear Steve:

...Anyway, if you're feeling blue on June 4th, my 4-H Beef Club is having their achievement date at 1:00. Come out and see your friends.

Signed, C.R.

Dear Steve:

If you are bored during the summer, we have a ball hockey league here. We need a defenceman for our team.

Signed, W.B.

Dear Steve:

Hey, it's okay buddy. Don't worry, everyone makes mistakes.

Signed, S.H.

Mike Eaves retired, unretired, and retired again in what could be described as the most and least memorable year in his pro hockey career. Eaves was able to play in a Stanley Cup season, and able to spend a season as a coaching understudy, his future career. It was forgettable because he was forced first to retire before his time, and then eventually retired because he wanted to. Unlike so many of his former teammates, who had the opportunity to bask in their winter's delight, Eaves did not. He left the Flames, the only player on the club to retire, to take a coaching position at the University of Wisconsin, Eau Claire. He left one busy time, and began another.

Eaves had always been a Johnson favourite, an example for others to follow. Players play better with Eaves on their line, the story went. And quietly, in all the noise of the playoff hoopla, he was gone.

"You know, you come into the league as a rookie, just trying to find your place," Eaves said in a mid-summer interview. "Then it takes you a few years and you find your place, you establish a spot and you belong. And just when you feel you belong, it's all over.

"I'm not sure how everyone looks at this, but we were given an experience of a lifetime. You spend your whole life looking for success, or looking not to fail. And then you find it. It's a hard feeling to describe, but I think our time was more enjoyable because of everything we overcame — the injuries, and the losing streak."

Eaves spent the season practicing, but not playing, with the Flames. And with it, he learned perspective. For him, it was easier to walk away, to leave the close friends behind, because he had prepared himself for that time. He had joined in on a Stanley Cup odyssey, but he was a rare athlete. He knew when to say goodbye. And he would remember everything.

"You look at the playoffs and you have so many memories," he said. "For me, coming back and playing was one, but there were others. There are moments, when you're out for a beer, that someone brings it up. And you get that feeling again. The feeling that you were involved in a chance of a lifetime. For me, it was almost a fairytale ending to a career, but it was more. Guys have asked 'What do you remember most?'

165

I remember the moment we beat Edmonton. I was up in the press box with Cliff (Fletcher) and Pierre (Page) and Glenn Hall and Coatsey (Al Coates). We watched the clock wind down and it seemed to take forever. We couldn't believe it. It was over, and yet we didn't really know how to react. I guess it's the same experience for the mountain climber who reaches the top. Your expectations of the moment are always better than the reality. We had done it, we beat Edmonton, and everyone looked at each other, as if to say, now what?

The circumstances of the Flames' success was ultimately unique. They had reached as far as they could go, despite so many setbacks — with a team few had expected or even considered capable. The playoff goaltender wasn't good enough when the regular season began. The health of their leaders had been constantly in question. The team had balance, but there were no scoring star; depth at forward, but not on defence. And then there were the college players. Teams can't win with college players. This is a man's game, where knowledge is learned from riding buses over frozen highways. But one by one, the myths were stripped away. The cant's became cans. Inexplicably it all came together, without reason, without explanation. It was like a magic show, now you see it, now you don't. And who knows what might happen next.

The only certainty is another season will begin and the players, for the most part, will be the same. But missing will be the spirit of Eaves.

"It's hard to leave good friends behind," said Eaves. "Deep down inside I knew it was time to move on and that's what made things easier. I felt fortunate just to have had the opportunities. Nothing in this game is ever easy emotionally. It's different from other jobs. You're together every day, you eat together, travel together, shower together. You wind up in situations where your emotions are hung out to dry. And you learn to deal with them.''

Steve Smith returned to Edmonton in early September, with a legacy he could no longer control. The Oilers were ready to begin another training camp, and he was again bidding for a regular spot. Mike Eaves was in Eau Claire, with few thoughts about the Flames, mapping out in his mind his first season as a collegiate head coach. Bob Johnson was in Calgary, again talking optimistically about taking another step forward: climbing Mt. Everest or Mt. Oiler — whichever came first. The rest of the Flame players were awaiting physical testing. Their lives had been changed in a matter of days, months, and hockey moments. It would never be the same again.

The Calgary Flames had written an amazing hockey story in the 1985-86 hockey season: shift by shift, chapter by chapter, month by month. It began in a Moncton training camp and ended eight months later on the streets of Calgary with a rousing parade. At the Stampede Grounds, the day the Flames were honoured, a fan held up a sign —

''Next Year Is Our Year.''

The Road to the Stanley Cup

Smythe Division semi-final   *Flames win series 3-0*
Calgary 5   Winnipeg 1
Calgary 6   Winnipeg 4
Calgary 4   Winnipeg 3 (OT)

Smythe Division final   *Flames win series 4-3*
Calgary 4   Edmonton 1
Edmonton 6   Calgary 5 (OT)
Calgary 3   Edmonton 2
Edmonton 7   Calgary 4
Calgary 4   Edmonton 1
Edmonton 5   Calgary 2
Calgary 3   Edmonton 2

Campbell Conference final   *Flames win series 4-3*
St. Louis 3   Calgary 2
Calgary 8   St. Louis 2
Calgary 5   St. Louis 3
St. Louis 5   Calgary 2
Calgary 4   St. Louis 2
St. Louis 6   Calgary 5 (OT)
Calgary 2   St. Louis 1

Stanley Cup final   *Canadiens win series 4-1*
Calgary 5   Montreal 2
Montreal 3   Calgary 2 (OT)
Montreal 5   Calgary 3
Montreal 1   Calgary 0
Montreal 4   Calgary 3

Calgary Flames Roster 1985 - 86

PLAYERS	HT.	WT.	PLACE OF BIRTH	DATE	1984-85 CLUB	1984-85 RECORD				
						GP	G	A	PTS	PIM
FORWARDS										
BEREZAN, Perry	6-2	192	Edmonton, Alta.	Dec. 5, 1964	U. of No. Dakota	42	23	35	58	32
					Calgary	9	3	2	5	4
BOZEK, Steve	5-11	175	Kelowna, B.C.	Nov. 26, 1960	Calgary	54	13	22	35	6
BRADLEY, Brian	5-10	170	Kitchener, Ont.	Jan. 21, 1965	London (OHL)	32	27	49	76	22
COURTEAU, Yves	6-0	194	Montreal, Que.	Apr. 25, 1964	Moncton (AHL)	58	19	20	39	32
					Calgary	14	1	4	5	4
EAVES, Mike	5-10	180	Denver, CO	June 10, 1956	Calgary	56	14	29	43	10
FOTIU, Nick	6-2	210	Staten Island, NY	May 25, 1952	New York Rangers	46	4	7	11	54
HUNTER, Tim	6-2	202	Calgary, Alta.	Sept. 10, 1959	Calgary	71	11	11	22	259
HULL, Brett	5-11	195	Belleville, Ont.	Aug. 9, 1964	U of Minn-Duluth					
LOOB, Hakan	5-9	178	Karlstad, Sweden	July 3, 1960	Calgary	78	37	35	72	14
McDONALD, Lanny	6-0	190	Hanna, Alta.	Feb. 16, 1953	Calgary	43	19	18	37	36
MULLEN, Joe	5-9	180	New York, NY	Feb. 26, 1957	St. Louis Blues	79	40	52	92	6
OTTO, Joel	6-4	220	St. Cloud, MN	Oct. 29, 1961	Moncton (AHL)	56	27	36	63	89
					Calgary	17	4	8	12	30
PATTERSON, Colin	6-2	195	Rexdale, Ont.	May 11, 1960	Calgary	57	22	21	43	5
PEPLINSKI, Jim	6-3	209	Renfrew, Ont.	Oct. 24, 1960	Calgary	80	16	29	45	111
QUINN, Dan	5-11	175	Ottawa, Ont.	June 1, 1965	Calgary	74	20	38	58	22
RISEBROUGH, Doug	5-11	183	Kitchener, Ont.	Jan. 29, 1954	Calgary	15	7	5	12	49
TONELLI, John	6-1	200	Milton, Ont.	Mar. 23, 1957	New York Islanders	80	42	58	100	96
WILSON, Carey	6-2	198	Winnipeg, Man.	May 19, 1962	Calgary	74	24	48	72	27

DEFENSEMEN

						GP				
BARTEL, Robin	6-0	200	Drake, Sask.	May 16, 1961	Moncton (AHL)	41	4	11	15	54
BAXTER, Paul	5-11	194	Winnipeg, Man.	Oct. 25, 1955	Calgary	70	5	14	19	126
JOHNSON, Terry	6-3	210	Calgary, Alta.	Nov. 28, 1958	St. Louis Blues	74	0	7	7	126
MacINNIS, Allan	6-1	193	Inverness, N.S.	July 11, 1963	Calgary	67	14	52	66	75
MACOUN, Jamie	6-2	197	Newmarket, Ont.	Aug. 17, 1961	Calgary	70	9	30	39	67
REINHART, Paul	5-11	205	Kitchener, Ont.	Jan. 8, 1960	Calgary	75	23	46	69	18
SHEEHY, Neil	6-2	215	Fort Francis, Ont.	Feb. 9, 1960	Moncton (AHL)	34	6	9	15	101
					Calgary	31	3	4	7	109
SUTER, Gary	6-0	199	Madison, WN	June 24, 1964	U of Wisconsin	39	12	39	51	110

GOALTENDERS

						GP	MINS	GA	SO	AVE
D'AMOUR, Marc	5-10	165	Sudbury, Ont.	Apr. 29, 1961	Salt Lake City (IHL)	12	694	33	0	2.85
					Moncton (AHL)	37	2051	115	0	3.36
LEMELIN, Rejean	5-11	170	Quebec City, Que.	Nov. 19, 1954	Calgary	56	3176	183	1	3.46
VERNON, Mike	5-9	155	Calgary, Alta.	Feb. 24, 1963	Moncton (AHL)	41	2050	134	0	3.92

1985- 86 Flames' Regular Season Statistics

PLAYERS	TEAM	GP	G	A	PTS	+/-	PIM
Joe Mullen	St. Louis	48	28	24	52	7-	10
	Calgary	29	16	22	38	3	11
	Total	77	44	46	90	4-	21
Dan Quinn	Calgary	78	30	42	72	12-	44
Lanny McDonald	Calgary	80	28	43	71	3-	44
John Tonelli	N.Y. Islanders	65	20	41	61	22	50
	Calgary	9	3	4	7	0	10
	Total	74	23	45	68	22	60
Gary Suter	Calgary	80	18	50	68	11	141
Al MacInnis	Calgary	77	11	57	68	39	76
Hakan Loob	Calgary	68	31	36	67	22	36
Joel Otto	Calgary	79	25	34	59	22	188
Jim Peplinski	Calgary	77	24	35	59	32	214
Carey Wilson	Calgary	76	29	29	58	1	24
Steve Bozek	Calgary	64	21	22	43	24	24
Doug Risebrough	Calgary	62	15	28	43	22	169
Perry Berezan	Calgary	55	12	21	33	19	39
Paul Reinhart	Calgary	32	8	25	33	4	15
Jamie Macoun	Calgary	77	11	21	32	14	81
Colin Patterson	Calgary	61	14	13	27	8	22
Neil Sheehy	Calgary	65	2	16	18	1-	271
Tim Hunter	Calgary	66	8	7	15	9-	291
Terry Johnson	St. Louis	49	0	4	4	6-	87
	Calgary	24	1	4	5	3-	71
	Total	73	1	8	9	9-	158
Paul Baxter	Calgary	47	4	3	7	5	194
Rik Wilson	St. Louis	32	0	4	4	9-	48
	Calgary	2	0	0	0	2	0
	Total	34	0	4	4	7-	48
Rejean Lemelin	Calgary	60	0	4	4	0	10
Yves Courteau	Calgary	4	1	1	2	1	0
Brian Bradley	Calgary	5	0	1	1	3-	0
Nick Fotiu	Calgary	9	0	1	1	3-	21
Mike Vernon	Calgary	18	0	1	1	0	4
Robin Bartel	Calgary	1	0	0	0	1-	0
Dale Degray	Calgary	1	0	0	0	1-	0
Mark Lamb	Calgary	1	0	0	0	0	0
Marc D'Amour	Calgary	15	0	0	0	0	22

GOALTENDER	GPI	MINS	AVG	W	L	T	SO
Mike Vernon	18	921	3.39	9	3	3	1
Marc D'Amour	15	560	3.43	2	4	2	0
Rejean Lemelin	60	3369	4.08	29	24	4	1
Totals	80	4850	3.90	40	31	9	2

1986 Flames' Playoff Statistics

PLAYER	GP	G	A	PTS	+/-	PIM	S	PCTG
Joe Mullen	21	12	7	19	3-	4	53	22.6
Al MacInnis	21	4	15	19	11	30	79	5.1
Lanny McDonald	22	11	7	18	5	30	70	15.7
Paul Reinhart	21	5	13	18	2-	4	34	14.7
Doug Risebrough	22	7	9	16	9	38	38	18.4
John Tonelli	22	7	9	16	3	49	44	15.9
Dan Quinn	18	8	7	15	0	10	34	23.5
Joel Otto	22	5	10	15	5-	80	41	12.2
Jim Peplinski	22	5	9	14	1	107	28	17.9
Hakan Loob	22	4	10	14	4-	6	56	7.1
Gary Suter	10	2	8	10	1	8	17	11.8
Colin Patterson	19	6	3	9	0	10	36	16.7
Steve Bozek	14	2	6	8	1	32	28	7.1
Jamie Macoun	22	1	6	7	8	23	42	2.4
Terry Johnson	17	0	3	3	2-	64	5	.0
Tim Hunter	19	0	3	3	1	108	7	.0
Perry Berezan	8	1	1	2	9-	6	6	16.7
Mike Eaves	8	1	1	2	5-	8	9	11.1
Carey Wilson	9	0	2	2	1	2	22	.0
Neil Sheehy	22	0	2	2	2-	79	11	.0
Rejean Lemelin	3	0	1	1	0	0	0	.0
Nick Fotiu	11	0	1	1	1	34	12	.0
Paul Baxter	13	0	1	1	4-	55	7	.0
Mike Vernon	21	0	1	1	2-	0	0	.0
Brian Bradley	1	0	0	0	0	0	2	.0
Yves Courteau	1	0	0	0	1-	0	1	.0
Brett Hull	2	0	0	0	0	0	1	.0
Robin Bartel	6	0	0	0	0	16	2	.0

GOALTENDERS	GPI	MINS	AVG	W	L
Mike Vernon	21	1229	2.93	12	9
Rejean Lemelin	3	109	3.85	0	1
Totals	22	1338	3.09	12	10

About the Authors

Eric Duhatschek, 30, is in his seventh year covering the Calgary Flames for *The Calgary Herald*. A vice-president of the Professional Hockey Writers' Association, Duhatschek joined the *Herald* in 1980 after two years with *The Albertan*. He is a regular contributor to *The Hockey News*, *The Sporting News*, and *GOAL Magazine*. He holds a Masters degree in Journalism from the University of Western Ontario and a Bachelors degree in English from the University of Toronto.

Steve Simmons is a sports columnist with *The Calgary Herald*, and has covered the Flames since 1980. Simmons, 29, is also a columnist with *The Hockey News* and has contributed to such magazines as *Maclean's, GOAL,* and *Hockey Illustrated*. Born in Toronto and educated at the University of Western Ontario, Simmons previously worked for *The Calgary Sun, The London Free Press* and *The Globe and Mail*. He currently lives in Calgary with his wife, Sheila.